BEGINNER'S GUIDE TO
CAKE DECORATING

BEGINNER'S GUIDE TO
CAKE DECORATING

MURDOCH BOOKS

CONTENTS

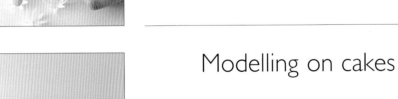

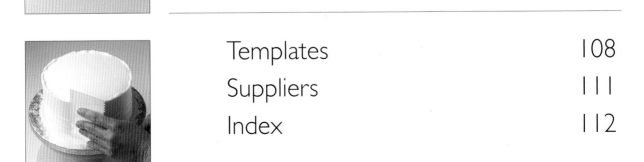

EQUIPMENT, RECIPES AND BASIC TECHNIQUES

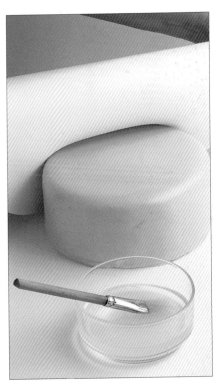

EQUIPMENT

Using the correct equipment not only helps to give better results, but also makes cake decorating easier. The following is a list of the basic equipment used in cake decoration. You will need specialist items to decorate some of the more elaborate cakes in this book, and these are listed with the instructions for each cake.

Cake boards

These are available in all shapes and sizes from round and square to heart, petal, hexagonal and rectangular. Choose between thin 'cards' and thicker boards or 'drums'.

Cake tins

Round and square tins are widely available in good hardware shops, kitchenware stores and even large supermarkets. Unusual shapes can be bought or hired from specialist cake-decorating shops. (See also Lining tins on page 10.)

Cocktail sticks (toothpicks)

These are useful for dotting tiny amounts of food colouring onto icing (see page 30), and for precise decorative work.

Tip

See the list on page 111 for suppliers of all types of specialist cake decorating equipment. Many of them supply goods by mail order.

Crimpers

These come in different shapes, e.g. hearts, diamonds, zigzags and scallops, and are used to emboss decorative borders and patterns in sugarpaste (rolled fondant) (see page 32).

Cutters

A vast range of cutters can be found in kitchenware stores and specialist cake-decorating shops. Large biscuit cutters are useful for shaping novelty cakes, while smaller cutters are better suited to more delicate work. Flower cutters come in basic petal

shapes, or are specially shaped for making particular flowers, e.g. orchids and lilies. Blossom 'plunger' cutters make simple flowers and have a wire spring which gently pushes out the flower shape once cut (for advice on how to use these, see pages 84-5).

Decorative scrapers

These are used for creating decorative patterns around the sides or tops of cakes (see page 67).

Dogbone tool

This tool has a large and a small rounded end, and is used for making soft curves on petals for sugar flowers. See photograph under Modelling tools, opposite.

Dusting powders

Powder colours are mostly used to give colour highlights to sugarpaste flowers (see pages 84–5). They are applied with a dry paintbrush.

Floristry wire

This is used for wiring flowers together into decorative sprays, and also for looping ribbons into sprays. It is available from cake-decorating shops and florists. Never push wires directly into cakes.

Food colourings

Food colourings are available in a variety of shades from cake-decorating shops and suppliers. Use paste colourings for deep or bright colours and liquid for pale colours. Dusting powder is brushed on to achieve subtle shades.

Frill cutter

This large cutter with a central detachable ring is used for making frilled borders and decorations. For full instructions on making frills, see Sugarpaste Techniques, page 31.

Icing ruler or straightedge

A smooth, firm ruler is used for flat icing the tops of cakes decorated with royal icing.

Kitchen papers

Plastic food wrap or cling film is useful for tightly wrapping icings to prevent crusts forming. Foil, crumpled or flat, acts as a mould for drying icing decorations. Greaseproof and non-stick papers are used for lining tins and for making paper piping bags and templates. Absorbent kitchen paper can be used to support sugarpaste decorations while they dry.

Leaf veiner

For marking leaf and petal veins, this provides a quick alternative to using the point of a knife.

Modelling tools

These come in various shapes and sizes and are useful for making all kinds of models to decorate cakes, from sugarpaste flowers (see pages 84–5) to marzipan fruits (see page 68). They are available from specialist cake-decorating shops.

Paintbrushes

Large brushes are used for moistening cakes or boards with water before icing, and for painting large areas of icing. Finer brushes are used for delicate painting, dusting on colour and for dampening icing pieces before securing to a cake.

Tip
Shiny new tins can reflect the heat, producing an uneven bake, so although you should wash tins after use, there is no need to remove the heat and baking marks.

Palette knife

This is useful for spreading or sandwiching cakes with buttercream, cream, chocolate or ganache.

Piping bags

Bought nylon piping bags are best for piping large quantities of whipped cream, buttercream or ganache. Homemade or bought greaseproof paper piping bags are used to pipe royal icing (see page 46).

Piping jelly

This is useful for adding a 'wet look' effect, particularly to water on children's novelty cakes.

Piping tubes (tips)

These range from very fine writing tubes, for delicately piped icing, to large tubes for piping shells, stars, basketwork, leaves and petal shapes. Very large star or plain tubes are available in sizes 5mm–2cm (¼–¾in). These are used with large nylon piping bags to pipe large amounts of whipped cream or meringue.

Ribbon

Lengths of ribbon are frequently used to decorate cakes, either in bows or loops on top of a cake, or tied around the sides. A ribbon attached to the cake board makes an effective finishing touch.

Rolling pin

An ordinary wooden rolling pin is adequate for rolling sugarpaste, although special plastic icing pins give smoother results. A small rolling pin is perfect for delicate work. Textured rolling pins are used to create fabric effects and other embossed patterns.

Sponges

Special sponges, soft and firm, available in various sizes from cake-decorating shops, are used when shaping or drying flowers. Pieces of sponge are used to support decorations while drying.

Stamens

These are available from specialist cake-decorating shops in a variety of shapes and sizes. They add the finishing touch to relevant flowers.

Sugarpaste gun or sugar shaper

This versatile piece of equipment creates pieces of shaped sugarpaste neatly and easily. A selection of discs provide different effects.

Sugarpaste smoother

A smooth, flat implement for giving a perfect finish to cakes covered with sugarpaste (rolled fondant).

Turntable

A cake turntable makes it much easier to work on a decorated cake.

LINING TINS

A wide variety of tins (pans) is now available for cake baking. Tins are not only designed to be a particular shape and size; consideration is also given to ease of use and how the baked cake will be removed from the tin. Nevertheless you should always make sure that all tins are well prepared beforehand.

Victoria sandwich (shallow) tins

These are usually used in pairs. Place one on a double sheet of greaseproof paper, draw round the base with a pencil, and then cut out the discs of paper just inside the pencil line (to allow for the thickness of the tins). Grease the tins with vegetable fat (shortening) and fit one of the discs of paper into the bottom of each of the tins, then grease the paper to aid easy release of the sponge cakes.

Deep cake tins

Measure the circumference of the cake tin first, using string or a tape measure. Cut a greaseproof paper strip, 5cm (2in) deeper than the tin and 5cm (2in) longer than the measured circumference. Fold up 2.5cm (1in) of the paper along one long edge, press to make a crease in the paper, then unfold. Grease the tin with vegetable fat (shortening) or melted butter. If you are lining a tin with curved sides, snip with scissors along the folded edge up to the crease. This will help you fit the paper neatly around the edge of the tin. For straight-sided tins, you need only snip the folded area when fitting around corners. Fit the strip around the outside of the tin. Place the tin on a piece of greaseproof paper, draw around the base with a pencil, and cut out the shape just inside the pencil line. Fit the shape in the bottom of the tin so that it covers the snipped edges of the side lining paper. Cakes that take a long time to bake, especially rich fruit cakes, need some protection to ensure even baking. Stand the tin on some newspaper, wrap a few layers of brown paper or newspaper around the outside and fix into position with string.

Moulded novelty tins

These cannot be lined with paper, so to ensure that your cake will not stick, first grease well with vegetable fat (shortening), and then dust liberally with plain flour. Knock out any excess flour before filling the tin with mixture.

If you are baking a large quantity of shaped cakes, or bake novelty cakes regularly, then a convenient method is to mix together equal amounts of vegetable fat and flour, and to brush this inside the tins. This mixture can be stored in the refrigerator.

CAKE RECIPES

If possible, always make non-fruit cakes the day before decorating them as they cut better: this is particularly inportant when shaping novelty cakes. Well wrapped in foil, a whisked sponge can be kept for two days before eating; a Madeira will keep for up to a week. Both should be frozen if kept for longer. Rich fruit cakes store well for several months in a cool, dry place. If liked, drizzle with a little brandy from time to time to improve the flavour.

Tip

When mixing a cake, curdling usually occurs because the ingredients are too cold. Make sure you start with everything at room temperature.

MADEIRA CAKE

1 Preheat the oven to 160°C (325°F/Gas mark 3). Grease and line the required tin (see pages 10–11).

2 Cream the butter or margarine and sugar together first in a bowl, until the mixture is pale and fluffy. Gradually beat in the eggs. Finally fold in the sifted flour using a large spoon and add any flavouring. Beat for about 2 minutes.

3 Turn the mixture into the prepared tin, level the surface then make a dip in the centre. Bake in the oven for the time stated in the chart or until the cake is firm to the touch and a skewer inserted in the centre comes out clean. Leave to cool slightly in the tin, then turn out onto a wire rack and leave to cool. Wrap the cake tightly in foil until you are ready to cover and decorate it.

MADEIRA CAKE

Round tin	15cm (6in)	18cm (7in)	20cm (8in)	23cm (9in)	25cm (10in)
Square tin	13cm (5in)	15cm (6in)	18cm (7in)	20cm (8in)	23cm (9in)
Butter or margarine, softened	125g (4¼oz/ ½ cup)	185g (6½oz/¾ cup)	315g (11oz/1⅓ cups)	440g (1lb/2 cups)	500g (1lb2oz/2¼ cups)
Caster sugar	125g (4¼oz/ ½ cup)	185g (6½oz/¾ cup)	315g (11oz/1⅓ cups)	440g (1lb/2 cups)	500g (1lb2oz/2¼ cups)
Eggs	2	3	5	7	8
Self-raising flour	185g (6½oz/1½ cups)	250g (8¾oz/2 cups)	375g (13oz/3¼ cups)	500g (1lb 2oz/4½ cups)	625g (1lb6oz/5½ cups)

FLAVOURINGS

Ground mixed spice	1 tsp	1 tsp	1½ tsp	2 tsp	3 tsp
Citrus (grated rind of lemon, orange or lime)	1	2	3	4	5
Chopped mixed nuts	30g (1¼oz/¼ cup)	60g (2¼oz/ ½ cup)	90g (3¼oz/¾ cup)	125g (4¼oz/1 cup)	155g (5oz/1¼ cups)
Baking time	1–1¼ hours	1¼–1½ hours	1½–1¾ hours	1¾–2 hours	2 hours

VICTORIA SANDWICH

Makes one 18cm (7in) sandwich cake
175g (6oz/³⁄₄ cup) butter, softened
175g (6oz/³⁄₄ cup) caster
(superfine) sugar
3 eggs (at room temperature), beaten
175g (6oz/1¹⁄₂ cups) self-raising flour

1   Grease and line the bases of two 18cm
(7in) sandwich tins. Preheat the oven to 180°C
(350°F/Gas mark 4).
2   Cream together the butter and sugar until it is
light and fluffy. Add the beaten egg in three stages,
beating well after each addition. If the mixture
starts to curdle, add a spoonful of flour with each
addition of egg.
3   Sift the flour onto the mixture, and fold in
gently with a large metal tablespoon.
4   Divide the mixture between the prepared tins,
and bake in the oven for around 20 minutes or
until the tops of the cakes are firm when pressed
with your fingertips. The cake should spring back to
shape and the fingermarks disappear.
5   Turn the cakes onto a wire rack. Peel off the
lining paper and leave to cool. Sandwich with the
filling of your choice. For an easy decoration, sift
icing sugar through a doiley, as shown below.

GENOESE SPONGE

Makes one 25 × 18cm (10 × 7in) cake
100g (3¹⁄₂oz/¹⁄₂ cup) margarine
160g (5¹⁄₄oz/1¹⁄₄ cups) self-raising
sponge flour
185g (6¹⁄₂oz/³⁄₄ cup) caster
(superfine) sugar
pinch of salt
2 eggs, beaten
100ml (3¹⁄₂fl oz/¹⁄₂ cup) milk
1 tbsp glycerine
a few drops of vanilla essence (extract)

1   Grease and line a 25 × 18cm (10 × 7in)
deep cake tin. Preheat the oven to 180°C
(350°F/Gas mark 4).
2   Put the margarine in the bowl of an electric
mixer with the flour, caster (superfine) sugar and
salt, and crumble together with your fingertips.
3   In a separate bowl, mix the eggs, milk, glycerine
and vanilla together. Mix at slow speed, and add
the liquid gradually over 1 minute. Scrape the
mixture then beat for 1 minute on medium speed.
4   Transfer to the tin and smooth flat with a
palette knife. Bake for 20 minutes or until golden
and firm. Turn out onto a wire rack, peel off the
lining paper, and leave to cool. Before using,
carefully peel off the top cake skin, as below.

VICTORIA SANDWICH VARIATIONS

CHOCOLATE
Replace 1 tbsp
flour with 1 tbsp
cocoa powder
and add 1 tbsp
milk.

COFFEE
Dissolve 1 tsp
instant coffee
granules in 2tsp
boiling water.
Add after
the egg.

ORANGE
Add the grated
rind of 1 orange
with the eggs.

LEMON
Add the grated
rind of 1 lemon
with the eggs.

VANILLA
Beat in 2 tsp
vanilla essence
with the eggs.

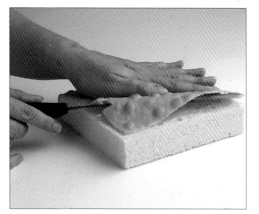

LIGHT FRUIT CAKE

1   Mix together the dried fruit, mixed peel, apricots and brandy. Cover and leave for several hours or until absorbed. Preheat the oven to 140°C (275°F/Gas mark 1). Lightly grease the tin and line the base and side, following the instructions on pages 10–11.

2   Beat the butter and sugar until combined. Gradually add the eggs, beating well after each addition. The mixture may look curdled at this stage. Transfer to a large bowl and stir in the sifted flour and spice. Stir in the soaked fruit. Spoon into the tin and smooth the surface. Tap the tin on the work surface to remove any air bubbles in the mixture.

3   Wrap a piece of folded newspaper around the outside of the tin and tie securely with string. Place the tin on several sheets of neatly folded newspaper and bake for the time stated in the chart. Using the chart as a guide, test the cake towards the end of the baking time. A skewer inserted into the centre of the cake should come out clean.

4   After baking, drizzle the cake with a little extra brandy if you like. Cover the cake with non-stick baking paper and foil, then leave it to cool in the tin for at least an hour.

5   When cool, remove from the tin, wrap in cling film and store in an airtight container until ready to decorate.

> **Tip**
>
> *If you prefer to use cup measures for ingredients, one cup is equivalent to 175g (6oz) of fruit or peel, 225g (8oz) of butter or sugar and 115g (4oz) of flour.*

LIGHT FRUIT CAKE

Round tin	15cm (6in)	18cm (7in)	20cm (8in)	22cm (9in)	25cm (10in)	28cm (11in)	30cm (12in)	
Square tin	12cm (4¾in)	15cm (6in)	18cm (7in)	20cm (8in)	22cm (9in)	25cm (10in)	28cm (11in)	30cm (12in)
Mixed dried fruit	250g (9oz)	440g (15½oz)	500g (1lb 2oz)	750g (1lb 9oz)	1kg (2¼lb)	1.25kg (2¾lb)	1.5kg (3¼lb)	1.75kg (4lb)
Mixed peel	15g (½oz)	30g (1¼oz)	30g (1¼oz)	60g (2¼oz)	90g (3¼oz)	125g (4¼oz)	140g (4¾oz)	150g (5oz)
Dried apricots, chopped	60g (2¼oz)	60g (2¼oz)	125g (4¼oz)	185g (6½oz)	250g (9oz)	315g (11¼oz)	370g (13oz)	435g (15½oz)
Brandy	40ml (1½fl oz)	40ml (1½fl oz)	40ml (1½fl oz)	60ml (2fl oz)	60ml (2fl oz)	80ml (2¾fl oz)	120ml (4fl oz)	160ml (5fl oz)
Butter, softened	160g (5¼oz)	250g (8¾oz)	315g (11¼oz)	440g (15½oz)	525g (1lb 3oz)	625g (1lb 6oz)	880g (1lb 15oz)	1kg (2¼lb)
Light brown or muscovado sugar	160g (5¼oz)	250g (8¾oz)	315g (11¼oz)	440g (15½oz)	525g (1lb 3oz)	625g (1lb 6oz)	880g (1lb 15oz)	1kg (2¼lb)
Eggs	2	4	4	5	6	7	10	11
Plain flour	185g (6½oz)	315g (11¼oz)	375g (13oz)	500g (1lb 2oz)	625g (1lb 6oz)	750g (1lb 10oz)	1kg (2¼lb)	1.2kg (2⅓lb)
Mixed spice	1tsp	1½tsp	2tsp	3tsp	4tsp	5tsp	6tsp	7tsp
Baking time	2hrs 5mins	2–2¼ hrs	3–3½ hrs	3½–3¾ hrs	4 hrs	4½–4¾ hrs	5–5½ hrs	5¼–5½ hrs

RICH FRUIT CAKE

1 Preheat the oven to 140°C (275°F/Gas mark 1). Grease and line the required tin (see page 11).

2 Cream the butter or margarine and sugar together first, then gradually beat in the eggs and fold in the flour and spice.

3 Stir in the mixed dried fruit, cherries and nuts until evenly combined.

4 Turn into the prepared tin and level the surface. Bake in the oven for the time stated in the chart or until the cake is firm to the touch and a skewer inserted in the centre comes out clean. Leave to cool in the tin.

5 Remove from the tin and wrap tightly in foil until ready to decorate.

Tip

When making cakes in hexagonal or similar shaped tins, use the same quantities of ingredients and baking times as those given for round tins of the same diameter.

RICH FRUIT CAKE

Round tin	15cm (6in)	18cm (7in)	20cm (8in)	23cm (9in)	25cm (10in)	28cm (11in)	30cm (12in)
Square tin	13cm (5in)	15cm (6in)	18cm (7in)	20cm (8in)	23cm (9in)	25cm (10in)	28cm (11in)
Butter or margarine, softened	125g (4¼oz/½ cup)	155g (5oz/¾ cup)	200g (7oz/⅞ cup)	280g (10oz/1¼ cups)	410g (14½oz/1¾ cups)	470g (1lb 1oz/2 cups)	625g (1lb 6oz/2½ cups)
Dark muscovado sugar	125g (4¼oz/¾ cup)	155g (5oz/1 cup)	200g (7oz/1¼ cups)	280g (10oz/1¾ cups)	410g (14½oz/2⅓ cups)	470g (1lb 1oz/2¾ cups)	625g (1lb 6oz/4 cups)
Eggs	2	3	3	4	6	8	9
Plain flour	155g (5oz/1¼ cups)	185g (6½oz/1½ cups)	250g (9oz/2¼ cups)	375g (13oz/3¼ cups)	500g (1lb 2oz/4¼ cups)	625g (1lb 6oz/5½ cups)	750g (1lb 10oz/6½cups)
Ground mixed spice	1tsp	1tsp	1½tsp	2tsp	3tsp	4tsp	6tsp
Mixed dried fruit	440g (15½oz/2½ cups)	625g (1lb 6oz/3¾ cups)	875g (1lb 15oz/5¼ cups)	1.1kg (2¼lb/6¾ cups)	1.5kg (3¼lb/9cups)	1.8kg (4lb/11¼ cups)	2.25kg (5lb/13½ cups)
Glacé cherries, chopped	60g (2¼oz/⅓ cup)	60g (2¼oz/⅓ cup)	90g (3¼oz/½ cup)	100g (3½oz/⅔ cup)	155g (5oz/1 cup)	185g (6oz/1 cup)	250g (9oz/1½ cups)
Chopped mixed nuts	30g (1¼oz/¼ cup)	30g (1¼oz/¼ cup)	45g (1¾oz/⅓ cup)	60g (2¼oz/½ cup)	90g (3¼oz/¾ cup)	125g (4¼oz/1 cup)	185g (6½oz/1½ cups)
Baking time	1½–2 hrs	2–2¼ hrs	3–3¼ hrs	3½–3¾ hrs	4 hrs	4½–4¾ hrs	5–5¼ hrs

CHOCOLATE CAKE

1   Preheat the oven to 180°C (350°F/Gas mark 4). Lightly grease the tin and line the base, following the instructions on pages 10–11.

2   Beat the butter, sugar and vanilla essence with electric beaters until light and fluffy. Add the eggs one at a time, beating well after each addition. Transfer to a large bowl and fold in the combined sifted flours, bicarbonate of soda and cocoa powder alternately with buttermilk.

3   Spoon into the tin and bake for the time given in the chart below. Insert a skewer and check it comes out clean. Leave to cool in the tin for 5 minutes before turning onto a wire rack.

RICH CHOCOLATE CAKE

Makes a 20cm (8in) round cake
110g (3¾oz) good quality dark chocolate
200g (7oz/⅞ cup) butter
200g (7oz/1 cup) dark soft brown sugar
1 tsp vanilla essence (extract)
4 large eggs
200g (7oz/1¾ cups) self-raising flour
pinch of salt

1   Line two 20cm (8in) shallow round cake tins and preheat the oven to 180°C (350°F/Gas mark 4).

2   Melt the chocolate in 3 tbsp water and allow it to cool slightly. Cream the butter and sugar until light and fluffy.

3   Separate the eggs and beat in the yolks, vanilla essence (extract), and then add the melted chocolate. Fold in the sifted flour and salt. Whisk the egg whites to a soft peak and gently fold into the mixture.

4   Divide the mixture between the prepared tins and level the tops. Bake for 20 to 25 minutes until they are firm to the touch. Cool in the tins before turning onto a wire rack.

Tip

The quantities given in the Rich Chocolate Cake recipe make a 20cm (8in) round cake. Double the amounts for a 25cm (10in) round cake and halve them for a 15cm (6in) cake.

CHOCOLATE CAKE

Round tin	15cm (6in)	18cm (7in)	20cm (8in)	22cm (9in)	25cm (10in)	28cm (11in)	30cm (12in)	
Square tin	12cm (5in)	15cm (6in)	18cm (7in)	20cm (8in)	22cm (9in)	25cm (10in)	28cm (11in)	30cm (12in)
Butter, softened	90g (3¼oz)	140g (4¾oz)	165g (5½oz)	185g (6½oz)	225g (8oz)	325g (11½oz)	465g (1lb 1oz)	560g (1¼lb)
Caster (superfine) sugar	165g (5½oz)	250g (8¾oz)	300g (11oz)	330g (11½oz)	410g (14½oz)	570g (1¼lb)	660g (1lb 7oz)	825g (1lb 13oz)
Vanilla essence	1 tsp	1½ tsp	2 tsp	2½ tsp	3 tsp	4 tsp	5 tsp	6 tsp
Eggs	2	2	3	3	4	5	6	7
Self-raising flour	40g (1½oz)	55g (2oz)	65g (2½oz)	75g (3oz)	95g (3¼oz)	125g (4¼oz)	150g (5oz)	190g (6¾oz)
Plain flour	115g (4oz)	165g (5½oz)	200g (7oz)	225g (8oz)	280g (10oz)	350g (12oz)	445g (1lb)	560g (1¼lb)
Bicarbonate of soda	½ tsp	¾ tsp	1 tsp	1½ tsp	1¾ tsp	2¼ tsp	2½ tsp	2¾ tsp
Cocoa powder	40g (1½oz)	60g (2¼oz)	70g (2¾oz)	80g (3oz)	90g (3¼oz)	110g (3¾oz)	120g (4¼oz)	160g (5¼oz)
Buttermilk	140ml (5fl oz)	210ml (7fl oz)	250ml (8fl oz)	280ml (9fl oz)	350ml (11fl oz)	500ml (16fl oz)	560ml (18fl oz)	700ml (23fl oz)
Baking time	50 mins	1 hr	1 hr 10 mins	1¼ hrs	1 hr 20 mins	1½ hrs	1 hr 40 mins	1 hr 50 mins

DARK GINGERBREAD

Makes about 24 pieces
410g (14½oz/3½ cups) self-raising flour
2 tsp ground ginger
½ tsp ground cloves
125g (4¼oz/½ cup) firm
unsalted butter
125g (4¼oz/⅔ cup) dark
muscovado sugar
125g (4¼oz/⅓ cup) black treacle/molasses
1 egg, lightly beaten

1 Preheat the oven to 200°C (400°F/Gas mark 6) and grease two baking (cookie) sheets.
2 Put the flour and spices in a food processor. Cut the butter into small pieces, add to the processor and blend until the mixture resembles breadcrumbs. Add the sugar, treacle/molasses and egg, and mix to a dough. Wrap and chill for at least 30 minutes.
3 Roll out the mixture on a floured surface. Cut out rounds or squares and place on the baking sheets. Bake for 12–15 minutes until the shapes have risen slightly and appear a little paler in colour. Leave for 2 minutes then transfer to a wire rack to cool.

CARROT CAKE

Makes a 20cm (8in) round cake
150g (5oz/1¼ cups) self-raising flour
150g (5oz/1¼ cups) plain flour
1¾ tsp ground cinnamon
¾ tsp ground ginger
½ tsp ground nutmeg
¾ tsp bicarbonate of soda
175ml (6fl oz) vegetable oil
200g (7oz/1 cup) brown sugar
4 eggs
100ml (3fl oz) golden syrup
450g (1lb) grated carrot
50g (2oz) pecans or walnuts

1 Preheat the oven to 170°C (325°F/Gas mark 3). Grease and line the cake tin.
2 Sift the flours, spices and soda into a large bowl and make a well in the centre. Whisk together the oil, sugar, eggs and syrup. Pour into the well, stirring, then add the carrot and nuts.
3 Spoon the mixture into the tin and smooth the surface. Bake for about 1 hour 35 minutes. A skewer inserted in the centre should come out clean. Leave the cake to cool in the tin for 15 minutes before turning onto a wire rack to cool.

ICING RECIPES

MARZIPAN

*225g (8oz/2 cups) icing
(confectioner's) sugar
225g (8oz/2 cups) ground almonds
1 large egg white
1 tsp lemon juice
a few drops of almond essence*

Marzipan or almond paste is used for both coating and decorative purposes. It forms a smooth coating on a cake – the perfect base for royal icing or sugarpaste (rolled fondant), and forms a barrier to prevent moisture from the cake seeping into the sugar coating. As a modelling medium, marzipan is easy to handle and pliable, and can be coloured by kneading in food colouring.

1 Place the icing (confectioner's) sugar and ground almonds in a bowl, add the liquid ingredients and stir together. Knead the mixture until smooth on a surface dusted with icing sugar.
2 Store in a polythene bag until ready to use. Use within a week of making.

ROYAL ICING

*25g (1oz) albumen (egg white) powder
¼ tsp lemon juice
500g (1lb 2oz/4¼ cups) icing
(confectioner's) sugar, sifted
1 tsp glycerine (only for cake coating)*

This is a traditional icing used to coat celebration cakes. According to the consistency (see page 46), it can be used for flat or peaked icing, or piping.

1 Place the egg white and lemon juice into a clean bowl. Using a clean wooden spoon, stir to combine.
2 Sift some of the icing (confectioner's) sugar into the bowl. Do not add too much sugar too quickly.
3 Using a wooden spoon, stir the icing sugar into the egg white and lemon juice, mixing well.
4 Continue mixing and adding small quantities of sugar until the mixture reaches the consistency of thick cream, then beat well until smooth and glossy. Stir in the glycerine, if using, then allow the icing to rest, covered with damp cling film.

Tip

There is a risk of salmonella poisoning when handling raw eggs, so make sure you wash your hands thoroughly after making marzipan and clean all the tools and surfaces used.

SUGARPASTE
(ROLLED FONDANT)

1 egg white made from dried egg albumen
30ml (1fl oz/2 tbsp) liquid glucose
500g (1lb 2oz/4¼ cups) icing
(confectioner's) sugar, sifted

Ready-made sugarpaste is easily obtainable, but this is a quick and easy icing to make. Once made, it can be coloured and used to cover all kinds of cakes. It is soft and pliable enough for making a variety of sugar decorations.

1   Place the egg white and the liquid glucose in a clean bowl. Sift the icing sugar into the bowl. Mix together with a wooden spoon until the mixture begins to bind together.
2   Form the paste into a ball with your fingers. If it is too soft and sticky to handle, knead in some more sifted sugar until firm and pliable.
3   Dust the work surface lightly with icing sugar and knead until the mixture is smooth and free from cracks.
4   To store, wrap the paste completely in cling film or store in a polythene bag with all the air excluded. If the sugarpaste dries out, knead in a little boiled water until it is soft and pliable.

MODELLING PASTE

280g (10oz/2½ cups) icing
(confectioner's) sugar
3 tsp gum tragacanth
1 tsp liquid glucose
315g (11oz) sugarpaste (rolled fondant)

This is one of the most versatile pastes for making models and decorations. Gum tragacanth acts as a strengthening agent, so that it sets much harder than sugarpaste and can hold its shape to make figures, animals, flowers and all kinds of models. For advice on modelling techniques, see pages 98–9.

1   Sift together the icing (confectioner's) sugar and gum tragacanth. Add the glucose and 6 tsp of cold water and mix well.
2   Knead to form a soft dough, then combine with an equal weight of sugarpaste. If the paste is too dry, knead in a little white vegetable fat (shortening) to make it soft and pliable. If the consistency of the paste is too sticky, knead in a little sifted icing sugar.
3   Roll out on a surface dusted with icing sugar. When modelling fiddly pieces (see pages 84–5), use a tiny smear of white vegetable fat on your fingers to prevent sticking.

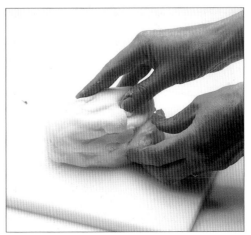

BUTTERCREAM

115g (4oz/½ cup) butter, softened
250g (9oz/2¼ cups) icing (confectioner's)
sugar, sifted
2 tsp boiling water

A versatile filling, icing or frosting for almost any type of cake, which can be spread evenly and patterned with a knife or scraper, or piped.

1   Place the butter in a bowl and beat until pale and fluffy. Add the icing (confectioner's) sugar a little at a time, beating well after each addition.
2   Beat in the water and any other flavouring if required. Alternatively, place all the ingredients in a food processor and blend for 30 seconds.

FLAVOURINGS

Vanilla – add 1 tsp vanilla essence

Citrus – beat in 2 tsp finely grated lemon, orange or lime rind

Coffee – dissolve 4 tsp instant coffee in the 2 tsp of boiling water before adding

Almond – beat 1 tsp almond essence and 2 tbsp chopped toasted almonds

Chocolate – beat in 30g (1oz) sifted cocoa powder or 50g (2oz) plain melted chocolate

Liqueur – add 3 tsp of your favourite liqueur

GLACÉ ICING

250g (8oz/2 cups) icing
(confectioner's) sugar
1–2 tbsp warm water
a few drops of food colouring (optional)

This quick and easy icing is used mainly as a simple topping for sponge cakes, and occasionally when making novelty cakes. Add the water cautiously as too much will give a very runny icing. If you work quickly you can produce attractive designs such as feathering (see page 63). This recipe makes enough to cover a 20cm (8in) cake.

1   Sift the icing sugar into a small bowl and gradually beat in enough water to make a smooth paste that thickly covers the back of a spoon.
2   Add food colouring, if liked. Use immediately, or cover with cling film to stop a crust forming.

FLAVOURINGS

Citrus – use lemon or orange juice in place of the water

Chocolate – stir in 4 tsp sifted cocoa powder

Strawberry – stir in a little pink food colouring and strawberry essence

Passionfruit – use passionfruit pulp in place of the water

FLOWER PASTE
(GUM PASTE)

400g (14oz/3½ cups) icing (confectioner's) sugar
50g (2oz/½ cup) cornflour (cornstarch)
3 tsp gum tragacanth or 2 tsp gum tragacanth and 2 tsp carboxy-methyl-cellulose (CMC)
5 tsp cold water
2 tsp powdered gelatine
3 tsp white vegetable fat (shortening)
2 tsp liquid glucose
1 large egg white (strained)

The paste required to make fine flowers and foliage is available commercially under a variety of names (e.g. flower paste, gum paste, petal paste) but you can make your own if you like. You will need a heavy-duty mixing machine with a beater attachment to produce a good result.

1 Sift the icing (confectioner's) sugar, cornflour (cornstarch) and gum tragacanth together into the bowl from your mixing machine, and warm. This can be done in a variety of ways: a metal or glass bowl can be placed in a low-heat oven; a plastic bowl can be put in the microwave on a warm setting; alternatively, place the bowl over a pan of hot water. In all cases, cover the bowl with a clean tea towel to stop the surface of the dry ingredients crusting, and warm the beater from the machine as well. Be careful not to make the ingredients too hot. They should be just warm to the touch.

2 Measure the water into a cup or small container and add the gelatine. Allow to stand for a few minutes to 'sponge', i.e. for the gelatine crystals to absorb the water.

3 Warm the gelatine mixture by standing the cup in hot water until the mixture is runny and clear.

4 Add the white fat and liquid glucose to the gelatine mixture and stir until the fat has melted. Use a wet spoon to measure the liquid glucose, or the spoon the fat was measured with, to prevent it sticking.

5 Add the gelatine mixture and the egg white to the warmed, dry ingredients, and mix on a slow speed until the ingredients are incorporated.

6 Turn the mixer to full speed and beat until the paste becomes white and stringy. If you hear the machine motor straining, turn the speed down a little.

7 Remove the paste from the bowl and immediately wrap in a polythene bag. Place in a small, plastic, lidded container, and place in the refrigerator to mature for 24 hours before use. For ease of use, wrap small pieces of paste individually before chilling.

> ## Apricot glaze
>
> *Warm 250g (9oz/1 cup) apricot jam in a saucepan until melted. Press it through a sieve, add 2 tbsp lemon juice, bring to the boil for 30 seconds then cool slightly. Apply to the cake surface with a clean brush.*

MEXICAN PASTE

*250g (9oz/2¼ cups) icing
(confectioner's) sugar, sifted
3 tsp gum tragacanth or gum tragacanth
substitute
2 tsp liquid glucose
6–7 tsp cold water*

This is a very elastic paste, which sets and dries hard. It is ideal for pieces that need to be strong or that will be handled more than usual.

1 Sift the icing sugar and gum tragacanth together on to a work surface and form a well in the centre. Add the liquid glucose and 6 tsp water. Mix all the ingredients together.

2 Add the remaining teaspoon of water if the paste appears dry or is crumbly. Knead well until the ingredients are well blended and the paste is smooth.

3 Place in plastic bags and seal in an airtight container. Store in a cool place for up to 6 weeks.

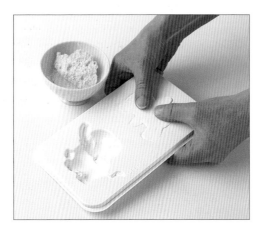

SUGAR GLUE

Sugar glue is used to stick pieces of sugarpaste (rolled fondant) together. Make it by mixing sugarpaste and water together to make a thick, brushing paste.

Alternatively, you can make a glue by mixing 5ml (1 tsp) gum arabic powder (available from cake decorating suppliers) with a few drops of water. Store in an airtight container in the refrigerator. Apply sugar glue with a paintbrush, using sparingly. Press in position, holding for a minute or two. If necessary, support with foam sponge until dry.

PASTILLAGE

*1 tsp gum tragacanth
175g (6oz) royal icing (see page 18)
75g (3oz/¾ cup) icing
(confectioner's) sugar*

The finest pastillage is made with royal icing and gum tragacanth. It can be rolled out finely, cut, shaped, curved and moulded to produce a variety of decorations, which will remain firm and strong. This is the strongest type of paste, so is often used for free-standing decorations.

1 Mix the gum tragacanth into the royal icing and leave to mature in a bowl covered with a clean, damp cloth for about 30 minutes.

2 Incorporate the sifted icing sugar into the mixture by mixing it in either by hand or with a heavy-duty machine with a beater. Immediately wrap in a polythene bag until required for use.

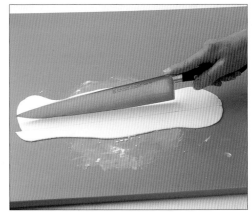

BASIC TECHNIQUES

COVERING WITH MARZIPAN

Marzipan or almond paste forms a smooth and flawless coating on a cake – the perfect base for royal icing or sugarpaste (rolled fondant) – and forms a barrier to prevent moisture from the cake seeping into the coating.

All-in-one method

This method creates a good base for sugarpaste and is suitable for all types of cake.

1   To obtain a flat surface to your cake, turn the cake upside-down. If the cake has peaked during baking or has an uneven surface, trim it level before turning the cake over. To avoid wasting too much cake, gaps at the bottom edge can be packed with small pieces of marzipan before the whole surface is coated.

2   Measure the cake across the top and down two opposite sides. Add 2.5cm (1in) to this measurement. Brush the top and sides of the cake with boiled apricot glaze (see tip, page 21).

3   Knead the marzipan into a smooth ball and roll it out on a work surface or non-stick board dusted with icing (confectioner's) sugar. Turn the marzipan occasionally to prevent sticking and to keep it roughly circular, until the

required diameter is reached, as measured in step 2. The thickness of the marzipan can vary according to taste.

3   Lift the marzipan away from the work surface, using the rolling pin as support, and lower it over the surface of the cake, placing the marzipan against the side of the cake first.

4   Smooth the marzipan, firstly across the top of the cake with the flat of your hand, then over the edges with your hands slightly cupped. Smooth the sides of the cake, again with the flat of your hand, and with an upwards movement.

5   Smooth the marzipan down to the base of the cake and trim off any excess with a sharp knife. Give the cake a final polish with the flat of your hands, then leave to dry or crust for a few hours.

Top and sides method

The top and sides are coated separately, creating strong (90°) edges suitable for coating with royal icing.

1 *For a round or square cake,* turn the cake upside-down and pack the bottom edges with marzipan to obtain a smooth finish. Brush the top surface with boiled apricot glaze. Roll out the marzipan on a work surface or non-stick board dusted with icing sugar until the marzipan is slightly larger than the cake top and the thickness required. Lower the jammed surface of the cake onto the marzipan and trim with a sharp knife. Turn the cake back over.

2 *For a round cake,* brush the sides with apricot glaze. Roll out the marzipan into a long strip and trim to the length of the circumference of the cake. Trim to the depth of the cake plus 1cm (½in), dust with a little icing sugar to

stop the marzipan sticking and roll it up. Unroll the marzipan around the side of the cake, trim to fit, and trim the top edge with a sharp knife.

3 *For a cake with corners,* brush alternate sides with apricot glaze. Roll out the marzipan into a rectangle slightly wider than the length of one side of the cake, and long enough to coat all the sides (i.e. four times the depth of one side for a square cake). Cut out the side pieces, making each one slightly taller than the cake and wider than its width.

4 Position the first side of marzipan and smooth into place. If a fold appears in the marzipan, lift it outwards and then gently ease it in again, smoothing downwards. Do not attempt to press the fold in, as this will result in an uneven surface.

5 Trim the top, cutting inwards towards the centre of the cake. Trim the marzipan to fit at the corners. Turn the cake and repeat, brushing with glaze when necessary.

COVERING WITH SUGARPASTE

Sugarpaste (rolled fondant) can be used to coat any cake. With a fruit cake, it is best to apply a layer of marzipan first. With sponge cakes, the sugarpaste can be applied directly to the cake, with just a thin masking of apricot glaze or buttercream. If you want to make different coloured sugarpaste, see page 30 for information on how to use colourings.

1 *For a fruit cake*, brush the surface of the marzipan with cool boiled water or clear alcohol (gin or vodka). *For a sponge cake*, brush the surface with boiled apricot glaze or spread with a thin layer of buttercream.

2 Before you begin, knead the sugarpaste with your hands in order to soften it (which will make it easier to work with) and give a smooth surface.

3 Measure the cake across the top and down both sides, and roll out the paste to 5mm (¼in), allowing an extra 2.5cm (1in) for trimming. Ensure that the sugarpaste does not stick to the work surface by turning it regularly as you roll it, using a dusting of icing (confectioner's) sugar.

4 Polish the surface of the sugarpaste with your hand to remove any excess icing sugar and to check there are no air bubbles in the paste.

5 Lift the paste over the rolling pin and use the rolling pin to position the paste on the side of the cake, over the top and down the other side.

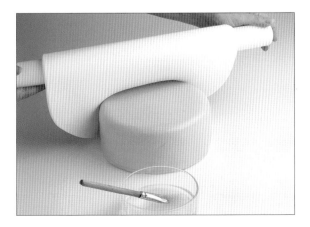

6 Smooth the top of the cake with the flat of your hand – it is best to start from the centre and work gradually outwards. This will ensure that you have not trapped any air between the sugarpaste and the surface beneath.

7 Work your way from the top of the cake down the sides, making sure that you are smoothing the sugarpaste down evenly as you go. As folds in the sugarpaste appear, lift the bottom edge out to remove the fold and then gently press the paste back onto the surface of the cake.

8 Continue smoothing downwards, using sugarpaste smoothers if you like.

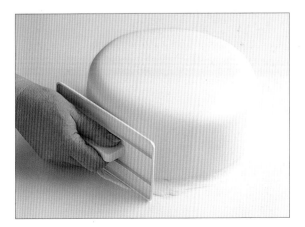

9 Using a sharp knife, trim away the excess sugarpaste from around the base of the cake to give a perfect finish.

COATING WITH ROYAL ICING

Royal icing is the traditional coating for formal celebration cakes. It provides a smooth, firm surface with sharply angled corners and edges. Coating with royal icing is, however, time consuming as the icing has to be applied in several coats and each coat must be left to dry before the next coat can be applied. An icing turntable is preferable when coating a cake with royal icing.

Three coats of royal icing should be applied to a marzipanned cake, leaving the cake to dry for about 8 hours between each layer. Use soft-peak icing for the first coat (see page 46), then add water to soften the icing slightly for the second coat, then soften again to apply the final coat.

Top coating a round or square cake

1   Place the cake on a turntable. Spread a little royal icing over the top of the cake with a palette knife. Hold the knife horizontally and work it backwards and forwards to eliminate any air bubbles in the icing. Spread the icing evenly to the edges of the cake, turning the turntable for even coating.

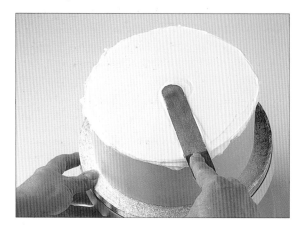

2   Remove the cake from the turntable and draw a clean straightedge or icing ruler (see page 9) over the top of the cake in one continuous movement to create a smooth finish. If necessary, wipe the ruler clean and repeat the process. Leave to dry before coating the sides of the cake.

Side coating a round cake

1   Place the cake on a turntable and start applying the royal icing to the side of the cake with a palette knife. Hold the knife vertically and position your finger at the back of the blade to apply pressure to the icing and disperse any air bubbles. Rotate the cake and paddle the icing as you work to form an even thickness.

2   Ensure that the icing covers the cake from top to bottom and that no marzipan can be seen. Use a plain cake scraper, pulling it round the cake in one smooth, even movement. When the scraper has been pulled around the whole cake, pull it off towards yourself to finish. If necessary, wipe the scraper clean and repeat the process.

3   This will leave a 'take off' mark which can be removed with a sharp knife or scalpel, using a scraping action. Neaten the top edge of the cake and the board with a palette knife before leaving the icing to dry.

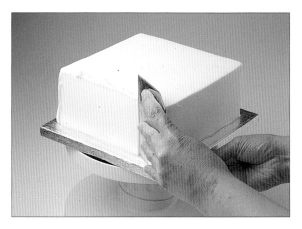

Side coating a square cake

1 Coat the first side of a square cake in the same way as a round cake. Move the scraper along the side, and at the end of the side pull the scraper off towards yourself.

2 Start the second side by bringing the 'take off' mark from the previous side round and onto the second side. Repeat this process until all four sides of the cake are coated. Always ensure that the edges are neat before leaving it to dry.

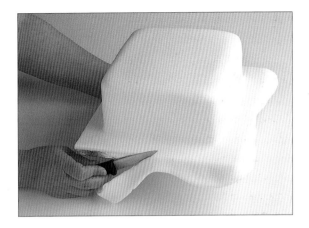

> ### Tip
> *The softer icing used for the final coat is much finer, and is easier to handle on the final coat if you scrape off most of the excess icing first, then repeat, pressing harder for a perfect finish.*

COVERING THE CAKE BOARD

It is common these days to coat the board with the same icing as the cake, giving the cake a neater appearance.

Covering the board with royal icing

1 Coat the board by paddling small amounts of royal icing onto it with the tip of the palette knife.

2 Use the palette knife at a 10° angle to smooth the icing on the board, again making a single 360° sweep. Clean off the board edge with the palette knife using a cutting down action and removing small amounts at a time. Clean the knife between each action. Wipe the edge of the cake board clean with a damp cloth. Leave to dry.

Covering the cake and board with sugarpaste

1 Place the cake on the board. Roll out the sugarpaste, allowing extra for the board. Lift the paste as if covering the cake, this time positioning the paste on the edge of the board first, then the side, top and opposite side of the cake, and finally, the far side of the board.

2 Smooth the sugarpaste from the centre of the top of the cake, down the sides and finally over the board. Trim excess paste away from the edge of the board with a sharp knife (see right).

Covering the board with a strip of sugarpaste

1 Coat the cake in sugarpaste as described on page 25, and place on a cake board (taking care not to mark the soft sugarpaste). Roll a sausage of sugarpaste with your hands, and then roll it into a strip with a rolling pin.

2 Use a tape measure or length of string to judge the length required. Trim the two long sides of the strip to the width required plus approximately 1cm (½in). Quickly roll up the strip, moisten the board with cool, boiled water, and then unroll the paste directly onto the board.

3 Cut the join to fit, and smooth the paste down with the pads of your fingers, particularly over the join. Trim around the board edge with a sharp knife. Finish by polishing the cut edge of the paste with the tips of your fingers.

Covering the board with centre removed

1 Coat the cake in sugarpaste as described on page 25, and allow to set firm overnight. Cut a paper template the size and shape of the coated cake. Brush the edge only of a cake board with cool boiled water. Roll out the sugarpaste and coat the surface of the board. Place the template where the cake will sit and cut around the edge with a sharp knife. Remove the template and the sugarpaste beneath it.

2 Lift the cake and lower it gently into the centre in the sugarpaste. Smooth the soft paste on the board into the join between it and the cake.

DECORATING
WITH SUGARPASTE

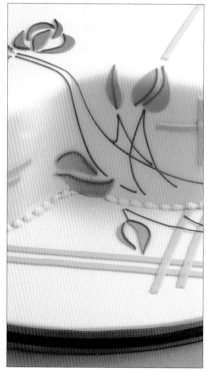

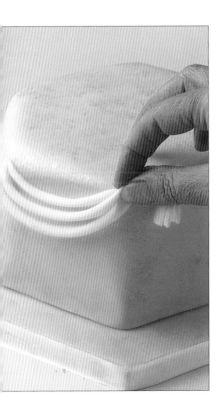

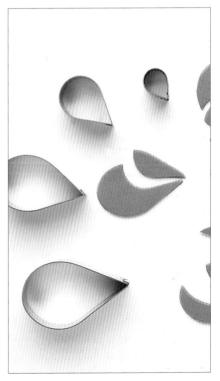

SUGARPASTE TECHNIQUES

Sugarpaste (rolled fondant) is pliable and easy to work with, covering cakes in one easy layer – it is used to create many cake decorations, such as realistic fabric effects, ribbons and frills.

Sometimes called rolled fondant or ready-to-roll icing, sugarpaste has now become very popular amongst both professional and amateur cake decorators. It can be used to coat any type of cake (see page 25) and can also be used in a number of decorative ways.

When freshly applied and still soft, it is the ideal medium for texturing techniques such as crimping and embossing, and many of the cake decorating skills adapted from needlework and other crafts, such as frilling and pleating, can be worked in sugarpaste to great effect. Once firm, sugarpaste provides a good base for piping and other finishing touches. Strengthened with gum tragacanth, the paste can also be used for modelling decorative shapes, and sets firm enough to be used for free-standing figures.

COLOURING SUGARPASTE

1   Weigh out the quantity of sugarpaste (rolled fondant) needed and place it on a surface dusted with icing (confectioner's) sugar, then knead it lightly until smooth.

Using a cocktail stick (toothpick), dot liquid or paste colouring onto the sugarpaste, then knead in until blended.

2   Always add colours sparingly as some are much stronger than others. For pastel shades, the paste might need only the smallest amount, while several additions of colour might be needed for deeper shades. Once the required colour is achieved, keep the sugarpaste tightly wrapped in a double thickness of cling film until ready to use (see also page 9).

MARBLING

1   This is achieved by only partially blending the colouring into the sugarpaste. Dot the sugarpaste sparingly with the chosen colour, as described above. Roll the sugarpaste into a long, thick sausage shape, then fold the ends to the centre and dot with a little more colour.

2   Reroll to a thick sausage and fold the ends in once again. Repeat the rolling and folding, without adding any more colour, until the colour starts to show in thin streaks. Add more colour, and repeat the rolling and folding process if stronger

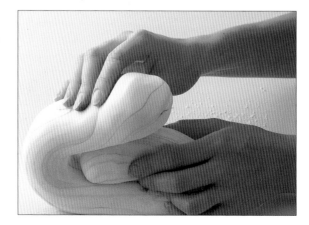

marbling is required, but take care not to overwork the sugarpaste, resulting in a uniform colour all over.

3 Once sufficiently marbled, roll out the sugarpaste and use it to cover a cake or board, as required.

FRILLING

Frills can be applied to the sides of a cake in a scalloped pattern or as a straight border around the base. Before making frills, make sure the cake is marked with template lines (see below) to guide the positioning of the frills.

1 Roll out a little sugarpaste (rolled fondant) on a surface lightly dusted with icing (confectioner's) sugar. If the sugarpaste is quite soft, you might need to strengthen it, either by adding 1 tsp gum tragacanth to every 450g (1lb) sugarpaste, or by making up a different paste that is 75 per cent sugarpaste and 25 per cent flower paste.

2 Cut out a scalloped circle using a frill cutter. Remove the cut-out centre.

3 Position the frill at the edge of the board, ensuring that it slides easily. Coat the tip of a cocktail stick (toothpick)

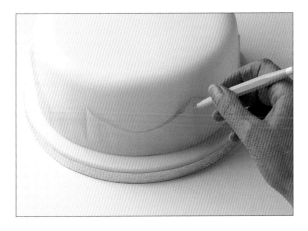

with icing sugar, and roll the tip along the fluted edge of the sugarpaste until the icing begins to frill. Use the side of the stick and not the point, to avoid making marks in the paste.

4 Continue to roll and frill all the way around, turning the frill as you go. Work quickly so the edge of the frill does not dry out and start to break.

5 Cut through the frill to make one long strip, and turn it over. Paint some cool, boiled water along the unfrilled flat edge. Lift the frill with both hands and line up the unfrilled edge along the marked lines on the cake. Cut the frill to the correct size with a scalpel, small sharp knife or fine scissors. Ease gently into position.

6 Use a cocktail stick to turn the ends of the frill under, allowing the frill to roll around the stick until the stick is at right angles to the cake. Lift all the pleats in the frill in this way until the overall effect is evenly distributed.

Tip

Some frill cutters come with adjustable centres so that the depth of the frill can be varied between 2cm (¾in) and 2.5cm (1in). Frills can also be made using a plain or fluted biscuit cutter about 9cm (3½in) in diameter. Cut out the centre with a smaller cutter.

31

CRIMPING

Crimping is a quick and easy decorative technique worked on sugarpaste or marzipan while it is still soft. A variety of different-shaped crimpers is available. The most widely used is a scalloped crimper, although straight crimpers, hearts, diamonds and zig-zags are also available.

Crimping can be marked along the top or bottom edges of a cake or along a scalloped template line marked around the sides. Crimping around the top edge of a cake as soon as the sugarpaste (rolled fondant) coating has been applied gives a quick, easy finish.

Crimping the bottom edge of the cake is a quick way of sealing the cake to the board, using an attractive pattern. Rope effects can be achieved by crimping lengths of sugarpaste positioned around the base of the cake (see page 33 for another method for making ropes).

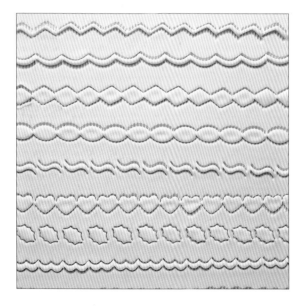

1 Dust the crimper with icing (confectioner's) sugar. Holding the ends about 5mm (¼in) apart, carefully pinch the icing, squeezing firmly until marked.

2 Lift the crimper away from the icing before easing the pressure or it will tear the icing from above and below. Repeat the pattern all around the top or sides of the cake.

EMBOSSING

Originating from leatherwork, embossing is very suitable for use on sugarpaste (rolled fondant) or marzipan. Many different embossers are available commercially and you can make your own embossing tools with carved buttons, jewellery, and so forth, but be sure to clean them well.

1 Coat the surface areas with sugarpaste and immediately start to emboss while the paste is still soft. When working along an edge, use the ball of your thumb to guide the embosser into the correct position.

Tip

To stop the crimper sticking to the sugarpaste, either dip the jaws into icing (confectioner's) sugar or wipe regularly with a barely damp, clean cloth. Alternatively, smear the jaws with white vegetable fat (shortening).

2 Textured patterns can be created by repeating the embossing technique in small areas. Enhance the embossed areas with colour, if required, using paste, liquid or powder food colourings mixed with clear alcohol and painted on with a fine brush.

MAKING A BOW

An icing bow is easier to assemble than one made from ribbon. The technique is always the same, regardless of size.

1 Colour some sugarpaste (rolled fondant) as required and roll it out thinly on a surface dusted with icing (confectioner's) sugar.

2 Cut out one long strip and two rectangles from the sugarpaste strip.

3 Dampen the ends and fold the rectangles over to form loops, tucking small rolls of absorbent kitchen paper or tissue paper inside the loops to keep them in shape.

4 Cut two more rectangles and pinch one end of each. Cut the other ends of these rectangles into V shapes to resemble ribbon ends.

5 Position the loops and bow ends on the cake so they almost meet in the centre, securing them with a dampened paintbrush.

6 Cut out a square of sugarpaste, dome it slightly in the centre, and position it over the centre of the bow to hide the ends. Secure with a dampened paintbrush, if necessary. Don't forget to remove the rolls of absorbent kitchen paper or tissue once the sugarpaste has hardened.

ROPES AND PLAITS

A simple and colourful finish for many cakes can be achieved by using sugar ropes and plaits, particularly on novelty and children's cakes. The most suitable medium is sugarpaste (rolled fondant) or marzipan, but fine ropes and plaits can also be made with flower paste (gum paste). Before applying them to the cake, dampen the bottom edge of the cake, or wherever you want them to lie.

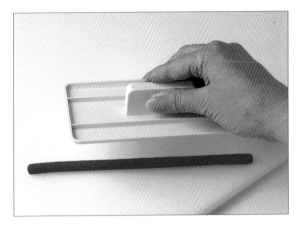

Twist – Thinly roll some sugarpaste on a surface dusted with icing (confectioner's) sugar to create a sausage shape that is 5mm (¼in) wide. Lightly twist it from the ends.

Rope – Thinly roll out two pieces of sugarpaste in contrasting colours under the palms of your hands. Twist the pieces together to form a 'rope'.

Plait – Use three colours of sugarpaste rolled out into very thin lengths, then 'braid', passing each strand in turn.

ROSE PETAL CAKE

This teardrop-shaped cake was inspired by the 1900s fashion for stylized flower decoration. By using different-sized cutters in conjunction, endless permutations of shapes are possible.

CAKE AND DECORATION

25cm (10in) teardrop-shaped cake

apricot glaze

1.25kg (2½lb) marzipan

1.25kg (2½lb) white sugarpaste (rolled fondant)

250g (8¾oz) mexican paste

250g (8¾oz/1 cup) royal icing

lavender, green, blue and pink paste food colours

sugar glue

EQUIPMENT

36cm (14in) oval cake board

ribbon cutter (FCC)

nos. 1, 1.5 and 2 piping tubes (tips)

piping bags

templates (see page 108)

scriber

tilting turntable (optional)

stainless steel rose petal cutter set (PME)

1 Brush the cake with apricot glaze and cover with marzipan. Coat with white sugarpaste (rolled fondant) and allow to dry for 24 hours. Coat the cake board with white sugarpaste and allow to set for 24 hours.

2 Divide the mexican paste into four portions and colour them lavender, pale green, pale blue and pale pink. Roll out and cut strips of paste with the ribbon cutter, or by hand, and fix them to the board with sugar glue, following the design.

3 Place the cake on the board. Using a no. 2 piping tube and royal icing, pipe a snail's trail around the base of the cake (see page 49).

4 Prepare the template (see page 108) for the top of the cake and trace the chosen design, showing the positions of the appliquéd flowers and leaves. Place the paper template on the cake and mark guidelines with a scriber.

5 Place the cake on a tilting turntable and tilt it away from you. Roll out and cut more strips of blue mexican paste with the ribbon cutter and fix to the sides of the cake with a little sugar glue, turning the cake as necessary.

6 Roll out pale pink and lavender mexican paste and cut out petal shapes. Using the different-sized cutters, cut the petals into shaped pieces, as shown below. Fix to the cake with sugar glue.

7 Cut out more petal shapes of green mexican paste and fix to the cake for leaves. Keep all the appliqué pieces as flat as possible with the edges clean and sharp. Press them gently into position without denting the paste.

8 Using deep lavender coloured royal icing and a no. 1.5 piping tube, pipe in the stems of the flowers and leaves. Using a no. 1 tube, overpipe the edges of the flowers and leaves.

The strips of coloured paste will look neater if cut with ribbon cutters.

Plan the shape of each flower before cutting it out and fixing it to the cake.

BRIDAL LACE CAKE

Any bride would be delighted to have a wedding cake decorated with the same pattern of lace as her dress. This can be achieved by using a piece of real lace as an embosser, a bought lace mould, or by making a mould from a piece of lace. Add a bouquet of sugar or silk flowers to complement the bride's bouquet.

CAKE AND DECORATION

30 × 25cm (12 × 10in) and 25 × 20cm (10 × 8in) oval fruit cakes

20 × 15cm (8 × 6in) teardrop-shaped fruit cake

2.75kg (6lb) marzipan

3.25kg (7lb) ivory sugarpaste (rolled fondant)

250g (8¾oz) white flower paste (gum paste)

mother-of-pearl dusting powder (petal dust)

sugar or silk flowers

1.5m (5ft) green ribbon, 15mm (¾in) wide

Tip

If making the mould, have all the materials ready before you start, because once the silicone compounds are mixed, they start to solidify fairly quickly and will only allow a short working time. Mix only the amount you need for the mould you want, as it is not re-usable.

1   If making a mould, cover a small work board with cling film. Mix together equal amounts of the two compounds supplied in the pack of Silicone Plastique (available from cake decorating suppliers), one white and one blue. Knead for a few minutes until firm, then roll it out onto the cling film to about 1cm (½in) thick (this will vary according to the thickness of the lace). Press the lace firmly into the paste, using a small sponge, paying attention to small details. Remove the lace and leave the mould to dry. It will be a few hours before you can use it. Alternatively, use a bought lace mould or impress a piece of lace directly into strengthened sugarpaste. (see step 7).

2   Place the largest cake on the cake board, the medium on the thin oval cake card, and cut the teardrop shape out of the thin square card using the cake tin (pan) as a template. Make sure the cards under the medium and small cakes are exactly the same size as the cakes, so that they do not show when the cake is coated.

3   Cover the cakes in marzipan. When dry, cover each cake with ivory sugarpaste (rolled fondant). Cover the edge of the base cake board with a strip of ivory sugarpaste and texture with a veining tool. Roll the tool backwards and forwards in short spans, keeping it at 90° to the edge of the board to make sure that the resulting lines radiate from the centre of the cake. Leave the covered cakes to dry for at least 24 hours.

4   Make a template of the top and middle tiers by drawing around the cake tins, then mark the positions of the dowels. There should be four dowels in the cake base

Remove the lace carefully and leave the mould to dry.

Texture the sugarpaste on the board with a veining tool.

SPECIAL EQUIPMENT

Silicone Plastique (CS) or lace mould
piece of lace
40 × 35cm (16 × 14in) thin oval cake board
25 × 20cm (10 × 8in) oval cake card
20cm (8in) square thin card
veining tool (HP)
7 cake dowels
sugarpaste gun and trifoil attachment (optional)
miniature cutting wheel (PME) or scalpel
wide flat dusting brush
cake pick

and three in the middle cake, due to the shape of the top tier. Place the templates on the cake below, and prick through to indicate where to insert the dowels.

5   At each point, make a hole in the cake with a narrow tool, then push the dowels straight down until they are resting on the cake card or board beneath. Mark the dowels level with the cake surface, remove, cut at the mark, and insert back in the holes. Position the cakes on top of each other. For safety, a small amount of softened sugarpaste can be spread under the cakes. Check that each cake is placed centrally on the cake beneath. Remember that the stacked cake will be heavy to carry.

6   Load a sugarpaste gun with sugarpaste and fit it with a large trifoil attachment. Extrude several long lengths of sugarpaste. Twist the lengths of paste and place around the base of the top cake, securing with sugarpaste glue. If you need to join two lengths, cut through both pieces at an angle and match the pattern. *Alternatively,* cut two long thin sausages of sugarpaste and twist them together (see page 33).

7   Mix equal amounts of sugarpaste and flower paste (gum paste) together. Roll thinly on a small board which has been lightly greased with vegetable fat (shortening). The fat will enable you to roll out the paste very thinly and ensures an accurate impression from the mould. Place the paste over the lace mould, with the fat side down, and press it firmly into the mould using a small sponge.

8   Remove the paste from the mould, turn it pattern side up and cut round the design with a miniature cutting wheel or scalpel. Brush with mother-of-pearl dusting powder and attach to the side of the cake with a little sugarpaste glue. Work with short lengths so it is easier to handle the lace pieces. Cut away part of the design to fill the gap when you reach the end of the cake circumference.

9   Make a hole using a length of dowel in the middle tier cake, just in front of the teardrop cake. Insert a cake pick and slot in a bouquet of artificial flowers, using a selection that will complement the floral arrangements at the wedding. Alternatively, make an arrangement of sugar flowers (see pages 84–5).

10   Attach a ribbon round the base cake board, either green or matching one of the colours in the bouquet.

Mark the dowel level with the cake surface, then cut it at that point.

Make a rope design by hand (see page 33) or using a sugarpaste gun.

Carefully cut around the lace with a miniature cutting wheel or scalpel.

BOWS AND DRAPES

Swags, drapes and bows give a soft, flowing effect to cakes, and strengthened sugarpaste easily folds into the shapes you require.

CAKE AND DECORATION

20cm (8in) round cake

apricot glaze

900g (2lb) marzipan

1.2kg (2½lb) sugarpaste (rolled fondant)

ice blue and mint green paste colourings

silver snowflake lustre powder

clear alcohol (gin or vodka)

1 tsp gum tragacanth

2 royal icing doves (optional)

SPECIAL EQUIPMENT

25cm (10in) round cake board

piece of sponge

paper for template

dowel rods or bamboo skewers

heart cutters

1 Brush the cake with apricot glaze and coat with marzipan using the all-in-one method (see page 23). Place it on the cake board.

2 Colour 800g (1¾lb) of sugarpaste (rolled fondant) with the ice blue and mint green colourings to make sea-green paste. Moisten the cake with cool boiled water and coat the cake and board in sea-green sugarpaste using the all-in-one method. Leave to dry.

3 Mix some ice blue and mint green colourings with silver snowflake dust and clear alcohol (gin or vodka) to the required colour. Tear a small piece of sponge from a larger block, dip in the colour and squeeze the sponge. Test the effect by dabbing the sponge over a spare piece of sugarpaste before applying to the finished surface. Once you are happy with the effect, dab the colour all over the surface of the sugarpaste, covering the whole area. Leave to dry.

4 To achieve a neat finish, it is important to use a template to show the position of the drapes, and to scribe this outline on to the cake. Using non-stick paper, make a template the depth and circumference of the cake and fold it into six equal sections. (This could be four, six or eight sections, depending on how many drapes you wish to have on your cake.)

5 Mark a curve on the top section of the template, then cut away the top part through all the folded sections. Attach the template around the cake with masking tape and transfer the curved outline on to the sides using the point of a scriber.

6 To make the drapes, mix 1 tsp gum tragacanth into 225g (8oz) sugarpaste. Measure the part of the cake across which the drape will be positioned and add 2.5cm (1in) to this measurement. Measure the width required, which will be

Cut out the measured drape with a sharp knife or scalpel.

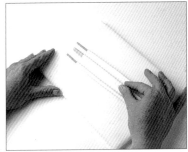

Place the drape over the dowel rods and ease the paste down and around them.

approximately 5cm (2in), and cut a rectangular template this size. Roll out the paste quite thinly and cut out the rectangular shape, using the template and a sharp knife or scalpel.

7 Lift the paste onto three dowel rods which are laid parallel 1cm (⅓in) apart. Ease the paste down and around the dowels. Remove the rods, leaving the paste in its curved shape. Pinch the ends of the paste together.

8 Moisten the surface of the cake where the drape will sit with a little cool boiled water or sugar glue. Lift the drape by the pinched ends only and gently shake it to encourage a curve. (The quicker the paste is folded, the less chance there is of the surface of the paste cracking, so practise several times before attempting to put the drapes on the cake.) Place the drape in position on the cake, following the curve marked with the scriber, and ensure it is firmly fixed. Trim away any excess paste.

9 There are six bows arranged round the sides of the cake. To make them, roll out some more paste strengthened with gum tragacanth, in the proportions given in step 6. Cut out two rectangles that are slightly smaller than those cut for the drapes. Use a dowel rod to shape the ends. Pinch the ends, then fold the paste in half lengthways and glue with cool boiled water.

10 Cut two tails from rectangles of paste and attach in position on the side of the cake. Add the bow loops. Cut a smaller rectangle of paste and lightly pleat by using a plastic skewer to lift it into folds. This will form the bow knot.

11 Moisten the position on the bow loops and wrap the knot piece around. Cut away any excess paste and rub the join smooth with a small modelling tool. *Alternatively*, make the bows shown on page 33.

12 Cut two larger hearts from white sugarpaste and attach to the top of the cake. Cut out and attach smaller hearts around the base of the cake.

13 Pipe dots around the hearts on the top and side of the cake and place and two shop-bought royal icing doves on top of the cakes, if wished. You could choose another decoration to replace the doves, such as tiny silk flowers or other suitable decorations.

Tip

Sponging is a useful technique to use when you need to make colour changes on a cake after the base colour has been applied. Fading effects are also possible, and sponging with masks, templates and stencils gives a wide range of decorative finishes.

Pinch the ends of the paste together and glue and shake it to make it curve.

Attach the drapes, following the outline scribed on the cake of your choice.

Make six large bows from strengthened sugarpaste.

CLOWN CAKE

Create this cheerful clown cake, using a simple technique to inlay pieces of sugarpaste (rolled fondant) around the side of the cake.

CAKE AND DECORATION

20cm (8in) round cake

apricot glaze

1kg (2¼lb) marzipan

icing (confectioner's) sugar for dusting

1kg (2¼lb) sugarpaste (rolled fondant)

selection of food colourings

ribbon to trim

SPECIAL EQUIPMENT

25cm (10in) round cake board

set of round cutters

sugarpaste smoother

template (see page 110)

carnation cutters

no. 0 paintbrush

Tip

Paint the clown's face with a fine paintbrush, using liquid colours or paste colours mixed with alcohol. Push sugarpaste through a sieve to make his hair. His trousers can be plain or painted.

1 Brush the cake with apricot glaze and coat the top and sides with marzipan, using the method on page 26 to obtain a 90° angle at the top edge.

2 Roll out some white sugarpaste (rolled fondant). Brush the top of the cake with cool boiled water and cover with sugarpaste, then trim the edge with a knife.

3 Roll out a sheet of sugarpaste slightly longer than the cirumference and slightly wider than the depth of the cake. Cut spots out of contrasting shades of sugarpaste and arrange them on the background sugarpaste. Roll the paste once in one direction then again in the opposite direction to even up the spots.

4 Brush the sides of the cake with cool boiled water and apply the spotted paste, fitting the bottom in neatly, trimming the join and finally trimming the top edge. Polish well with a smoother and leave to dry before placing the cake on the cake board. Cover the board using the strip method (see page 27).

5 Make the template for the clown (see page 110). The base is cut out as one piece of white sugarpaste and the clothing and body added afterwards. To create stripes or checks for the clown's trousers, roll out the base colour sugarpaste, then roll out paste thinly in a contrasting colour and cut into strips or small squares. Moisten slightly and place on the base colour sugarpaste, arranging in stripes or in a chequered design. Roll over in both directions then cut as desired. (See also tip.) Use carnation cutter sizes to make the ruffs. Assemble the clown as shown.

6 Attach a twisted rope of sugarpaste (see page 33) to the bottom edge of the cake with a little cool boiled water. To make the top 'circus ring', roll a length of sugarpaste and form it into a ring. Smooth the join. Moisten the top edge of the cake and position the ring. Attach the ribbon around the board.

Inlay work can be created using all different shapes and colours.

Roll red- and yellow-coloured sugarpaste to make the rope around the base.

DECORATING WITH
ROYAL ICING

ROYAL ICING TECHNIQUES

Royal-iced cakes with classic 'flat' surfaces and delicate piping are traditionally reserved for weddings and very special occasions. Such cakes are more time-consuming to make than novelty or sugarpaste (rolled fondant) cakes, but achieving a good result is extremely rewarding. With practice, piped designs make the most beautiful finishes.

There are two terms used to describe the consistency of royal icing: soft peak and full peak. *Soft peak* is the first consistency reached during beating and is used for coating a cake. Icing should retain a peak that will hold its shape but not be stiff and over-firm. *Full peak* is a stiffer, firmer consistency, leaving a definite bold peak. Use this icing for piping. Almost all border designs derive from basic tube (tip) aperture shapes. To pipe border work you will need a fair amount of icing. Fill the bag two-thirds full. Fold over the top of the bag, and hold the bag firmly in one hand as you pipe. Piping tubes (tips) are available in a huge range of sizes, both plain and shaped for special purposes.

MAKING A PAPER PIPING BAG

1 Cut a 25cm (10in) square of greaseproof paper, then cut the square in half diagonally to make two triangles. Holding one triangle with its longest side away from you, fold the right-hand point over to meet the bottom point, curling the paper round to make a cone shape.

2 Fold the left-hand point over the cone and bring all three points together.

3 Fold the points over twice to secure. Cut off 1cm (½in) of the tip and fit with a piping tube. Fill the bag half to two-thirds full with royal icing. Seal the piping bag by first folding the sides then fold the top down.

USING PIPING TUBES

To pipe straight lines, fit a piping bag with a small plain tube (tip) and fill with royal icing. For best results, hold the bag using the first finger of the right hand to support the bag underneath, while the thumb of the right hand keeps the bag closed at the top and applies pressure on the icing to force it through the tube. The action of pressing the icing through the bag will inevitably make your hand shake a little, so use the first finger of your left hand to steady the bag. By holding your finger against the bag, you can use it to stop your other hand shaking during piping.

I   Touch the tube down onto the surface and start squeezing the bag.

2   Lift the tube, allowing icing to extrude in a straight line. To keep a straight line, stretch the icing slightly, still squeezing.

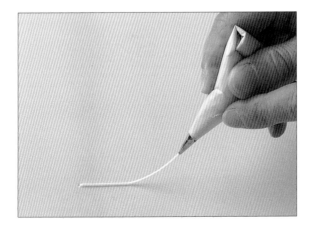

3   As the end of the line is almost reached, lower the tube to the surface, easing off the pressure. Touch the tube down, stop squeezing and lift off.

Shells

Use tube (tip) nos. 5, 7, 9, 11, 12, 13 or 15. Position the tube and apply pressure with your thumb to extrude a bulb of icing, then slowly and gently ease the bag back to form a 'tail'. Position the bag to pipe the next shell so that it just touches the tail of the previous one.

Alternating shells

Use small (nos. 5, 7 or 9) or large (nos. 11, 12 or 13) star tube (tip). Use the same technique as for shells, but pipe on either side of an imaginary line (using the top edge or base of the cake as the line) from left to right, bringing the tails into the centre at an angle of about 45 degrees. Start with the second shell slightly lower than the first, then continue piping so that each shell piped just touches the previous one.

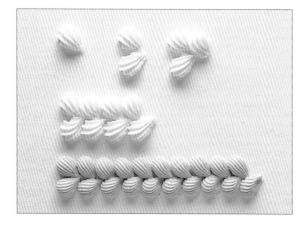

Bulbs

Use a piping tube (tip) no. 3 or 4. Piping bulbs involves holding the piping bag in a slightly different way to shell piping. Two-thirds fill a bag with slightly softened icing (add a few drops of cold water) – not runny but firm enough to retain its shape when piped. Position the tube, holding the bag almost upright, as shown. Keep the tube slightly away from the cake surface and apply pressure to the bag to extrude the icing. Keeping the tube in and below the surface of the bulb, continue piping steadily, lifting the tube slightly all the time until the desired bulb shape is formed. To remove the tube, lift it level to the surface of the bulb and using a quick but fairly accurate sideways movement, make the icing level. If necessary, use a paintbrush to 'blend' the cut-off mark.

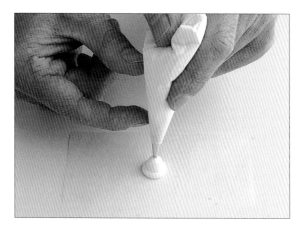

Stars

Use star tube (tip) nos. 5, 7, 9, 11, 12, 13 or 15. Hold the bag upright, forcing the icing out to the size of star required then pull up to form a point.

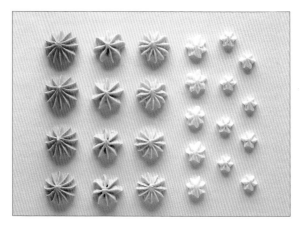

Twisted rope

Use plain writing tube (tip) nos. 2, 3 or 4, or rope tube (tip) nos. 42, 43 or 44, or star tube (tip) nos. 5, 7, 8, 11, 12, 13 or 15. Position the tube and press to extrude the icing. Keeping a constant pressure and speed, twist the bag as you pipe in a clockwise or anti-clockwise circular motion.

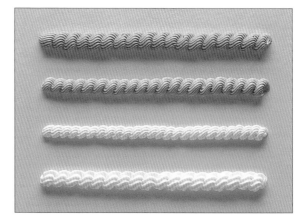

PIPED FLOWERS

Piped flowers make a pretty addition to any cake. Use petal piping tubes and stiff royal icing. If available, add a few drops of acetic acid to the royal icing; this will make it stronger and the petals will 'break away' more easily when piped. Most piped flowers are made on a flower nail, with small squares of greaseproof paper stuck to the nail with icing.

To pipe simple flowers

1   Use a no. 57 tube (tip). Lay the thick end of the tube on the centre of the flower nail. Lift the thin end of the tube up slightly (approximately 20°), and pipe the first petal using an upwards and downwards movement with the tube touching the surface of the paper. At the same time, turn the flower nail in an anti-clockwise direction (for right-handed piping) or clockwise direction (for left-handed).

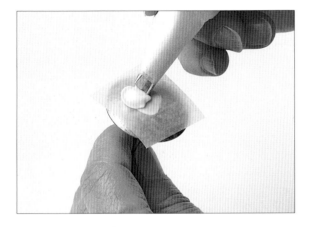

2   Tuck the tube underneath the first petal and repeat the action.

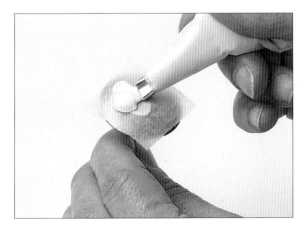

3   Continue this process until you have completed six petals. When piping the final petal, lift the icing up over the first petal.

4   Make the centre, piping a series of small yellow dots with a no. 1 tube (tip).

5   The flower can be removed from the nail, on its square of paper, while still soft.

Snail's trail

Snail's trail is the name given to a continuous line of royal icing piped dots usually edging the base of a cake. The piping bag is not lifted away between each dot, just moved along slightly, although the pressure is stopped until the next dot is piped.

FLORAL BASKETWEAVE CAKE

Decorated with piped basketwork and an abundance of fresh, artificial or sugar flowers, this stacked wedding cake is one of the easiest, yet most stunning, cakes to make.

CAKE AND DECORATION

28cm (11in), 20cm (8in) and 13cm (5in) round rich fruit cakes

apricot glaze

3kg (6½lb) marzipan

icing (confectioner's) sugar for dusting

1kg (2¼lb) soft peak royal icing (see page 46)

cream food colouring

1kg (2¼lb) full peak royal icing (see page 46)

fresh, silk or sugar flowers

SPECIAL EQUIPMENT

23cm (9in) and 15cm (6in) round silver cake cards

33cm (13in) round silver cake board

paper piping bags

medium writing tube (tip)

basketwork tube

medium star tube

1   Brush the cakes with apricot glaze and cover with marzipan. Allow 500g (1lb 2oz) paste for the small cake, and position it on the small cake card. Allow another 1kg (2¼lb) for the middle cake and place it on the large cake card. Use the remaining marzipan for the large cake and position it on the cake board.

2   Colour the royal icing for flat icing pale cream. Cover each tier with one layer of flat icing, and leave to harden overnight.

3   Colour the royal icing for decoration pale cream to create the basketwork piping on all three cakes. Fit one piping bag with a medium writing tube, and another with a basketwork tube. First pipe a straight line over the area of the cake to be covered. Using the basketwork tube, pipe 2.5cm (1in) bands of icing, a tube-width apart, over the piped line. Pipe a second line, just touching the ends of the basketwork, starting at the first line and crossing over the second line in the same way.

4   Spread the centre of the largest cake with a little of the remaining royal icing, then gently rest the middle tier over it. Spread the centre of the middle tier with a little icing, then place the small tier in position.

5   Using a medium star tube, pipe a border of shells around the bases of the top and middle tiers. Pipe further rows of shells around the edge of each tier. Leave to harden for at least 24 hours. The cake can then be stored for up to 2 weeks.

6   Decorate each tier with fresh, silk or sugar flowers. Snip the fresh stems to 6cm (2½in) long and position them around the tiers, overlapping so that each stem is covered by the next flower. Arrange the fresh, silk or sugar flowers as close to the time of the reception as possible. Make sure the fresh flowers you use are suitable for using with food. If you prefer, you can wrap the stems in cling film.

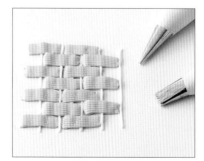

Basketwork, created by using writing and basketwork tubes, can cover large areas.

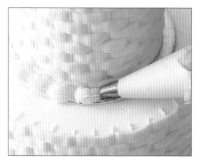

See page 47 for instructions on piping shell borders around cake bases.

COMING-OF-AGE CAKE

Gold-edge filigree work gives an interesting finish to this unusual 18th- or 21st-birthday celebration cake.

CAKE AND DECORATION

28cm (11in) square rich fruit cake

4 tbsp apricot glaze

2kg (4½lb) marzipan

icing (confectioner's) sugar for dusting

2kg (4½lb) sugarpaste (rolled fondant)

blue, green and gold food colourings

500g (1lb 2oz) royal icing

2m (6½ft) gold or coloured ribbon, about 3cm (1¼in) wide

SPECIAL EQUIPMENT

33cm (13in) square gold cake board

2 paper piping bags

fine writing tube (tip)

medium star piping tube

fine paintbrush

key template (see page 108)

1 Brush the cake with apricot glaze and cover with marzipan. Place on the cake board and dust the top with icing (confectioner's) sugar, to within 2.5cm (1in) of the edges. Cut out a 23cm (9in) square of greaseproof or non-stick paper.

2 Roll out the sugarpaste (rolled fondant) on a surface dusted with icing sugar and use to cover the cake. Reserve the trimmings. Lay the square of greaseproof paper over the top, securing it at the corner with pins. Using a sharp knife, cut right through the sugarpaste around the paper. Lift out the central square of white sugarpaste and remove the paper and pins.

3 Knead the white sugarpaste square and trimmings together and colour with equal quantities of blue and green colourings. Roll out and cut a 23cm (9in) square, reserving the trimmings. Lay the square over the top of the cake, so that the edges meet the edges of the white icing. Smooth down lightly.

4 Use the coloured icing trimmings to make the key, using the template on page 108 to cut out the shape. Leave to harden overnight.

5 Put a little royal icing in a piping bag fitted with a fine writing tube, and pipe thin wavy lines (cornelli work) over about two-thirds of the coloured icing. Using royal icing and a medium star tube, pipe a shell border (see page 47) around the edge of the coloured icing and the base of the cake. Leave overnight.

6 Using gold food colouring and a fine paintbrush, carefully paint over the piped icing and paint the edges of the key. Leave to dry for several hours.

7 Wrap the ribbon around the sides of the cake, securing with a dot of royal icing. Shape the remaining ribbon into a bow and position it on top of the cake. Lay the key over the bow fixing both with a small dot of royal icing if necessary.

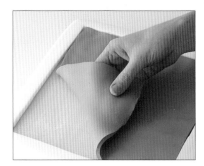

Lay the square of coloured sugarpaste over the top, butting up to the edges.

Carefully paint gold food colouring over the piped wavy lines.

GINGERBREAD COTTAGE

*Often associated with the characters Hansel and Gretel, this gingerbread house
makes a good cake alternative for a winter birthday or Christmas party.*

CAKE AND DECORATION

dark gingerbread mixture
(see page 17)

225g (8oz) royal icing

10 small ratafia biscuits
(cookies)

85g (3oz) chocolate-covered
raisins

approx. 15–18 chocolates or
small truffles

small packet candy-covered
chocolates

7 small, square wafer-thin
chocolate biscuits (cookies)

1 small chocolate-covered
fudge bar, thinly sliced

SPECIAL EQUIPMENT

2 baking (cookie) sheets

templates (see page 109)

4cm (1½in) round cutter

paper piping bag

board or rectangular plate,
about 28 x 20cm (11 x 8in)

1 Preheat the oven to 200°C (400°F/Gas mark 6) and grease two baking (cookie) sheets. Trace the templates on page 109 onto sheets of paper and cut out.

2 To make the gingerbread, put the flour and spices in a food processor. Cut the butter into small pieces, add to the processor and blend until the mixture resembles breadcrumbs. Add the sugar, treacle/molasses and egg, and mix to a dough. Wrap and chill for at least 30 minutes.

3 Thinly roll out the dark gingerbread mixture (see page 17) on a floured surface and cut out the cottage shapes. Use the template to cut out a door from the front of the cottage and then trim 5mm (¼in) off the base of the door. Cut out a window from the area above the door using the 4cm (1½in) round cutter.

4 Transfer all the pieces to the baking sheets, including the door, and bake for about 15 minutes until slightly risen. Leave the pieces on the tray for 2 minutes before transferring them to a wire rack.

5 Spread a little icing along the base and up the sides of one side section. Spread more icing along the base of the front section and secure the two sections together on the board, propping up the biscuits with small glasses or tumblers for support until they have set.

6 Secure the back section, then the other side, and leave for about 30 minutes to set slightly.

7 Before positioning the second section of the roof, you could fill the house with chocolate and sweet treats for an extra surprise.

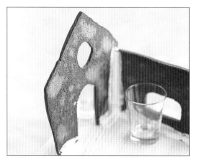

Spread icing along the base and up the sides of the house.

Secure the pieces together with icing and prop them up until they set.

Tip

*You could make a tiny figure
to stand in the doorway
of the gingerbread house.
See pages 98–9 for instructions
on modelling figures.*

8 Spread more icing over the top edges of the side pieces and secure one of the roof sections, again using glasses or tumblers to give the shapes support. Then spread a little icing along the top of the roof and secure the other piece in place and allow it to dry.

9 Using a palette knife or metal spatula, spread a thin layer of icing over the roof. If the icing feels stiff and will not spread easily, thin it with a little water.

10 For the icicles, hold a teaspoon of icing at an angle above the edges of the roof. As the icing starts to slip from the spoon, catch it along the edges, to create the impression of dangling icicles. (Again, if the icing is too stiff, thin it with a little water first.)

11 Use the small ratafia biscuits (cookies), chocolates or small truffles and chocolate-covered raisins and candies to decorate the roof. The pieces can be positioned randomly, but add a single row of chocolate raisins along the top of the roof for the top tiles.

12 Spoon a little more icing into the piping bag and put this aside for later use. Then spread the remaining icing over the board, swirling and lifting it in peaks with a palette knife or the back of a spoon to look like snow on the ground.

13 Pipe a little royal icing onto the backs of the square chocolate biscuits and secure them on either side of the window. Arrange the remaining biscuits at the front of the cottage so that you create the impression of doorsteps leading up to the house.

14 Pipe a line of icing around the door arch and press the door in position. Decorate the window ledges and round window with chocolate-covered raisins, securing each into position with a dab of icing. Secure another raisin for the doorknob and place a few candy-covered disks on the royal iced board to suggest a path.

15 Use the icing in the bag to pipe decorative edges around the door and along the corners of the cottage. Depending on your skill level, you can pipe dots, shells or a rope effect (see pages 47–8). Add small chocolate fudge slices around the base.

Use a teaspoon to dangle icicles of icing over the edge of the roof.

Position the door shape that was cut out in step 3.

Pipe decorative edges around the door and down the corners of the cottage.

FLOODWORK FLOWERS

Transform a simple cake into a work of art, using the floodwork or run out technique. All you need is a palette of coloured icing and a little imagination.

CAKE AND DECORATION

1 egg white

350g (12oz/3 cups) icing (confectioner's) sugar

3 tsp lemon juice

assorted food colourings

80ml (2¾fl oz) cream

150g (5oz) white chocolate

200g (7oz/⅞ cup) unsalted butter

18 x 25cm (7 x 10in) oval chocolate cake or cake of your choice

SPECIAL EQUIPMENT

flower template (see page 110)

1mm piping tube (tip)

paper piping bags

serving plate

1   Firstly, you need to make the flowers. Start by lightly beating the egg white with a wooden spoon. Gradually add 250g (9oz) of sifted icing (confectioner's) sugar and beat until you have a smooth paste. Then add 2 tsp lemon juice slowly until the mixture has a slightly stiff piping consistency – ensure that it is not too runny or it will become extremely difficult to work with. Cover the surface of the mixture with cling film straight away to prevent it from drying out.

2   Draw 16 simple flowers from the flower template on a sheet of blank paper and tape it to a flat work surface. Alternatively, you could design your own flower shapes if you like. Tape a sheet of baking paper over the top of the drawing sheet.

3   Using a piping bag fitted with a 1mm piping tube (tip), pipe carefully over the outlines of the flowers. Remove the baking paper sheet and set aside to dry. Repeat the process with a second sheet of baking paper or until you have made enough flowers to decorate the cake.

4   Gradually add more lemon juice to the icing until it is slightly thinner and is easy to spread smoothly. Divide the icing into four bowls and add a different food colouring to each, such as pale blue, pink and yellow, which are the colours used for this cake. Ensure that you keep the bowls covered or the icing will dry out.

5   Using paper piping bags, pipe or 'flood' the coloured icing inside the flower outlines and in the flower centres, moving the bag slowly backwards

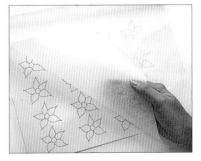

Draw the flowers on paper, tape to a surface and cover with baking paper.

Pipe white icing carefully around the outlines of the flowers.

and forwards using a little pressure to ease the icing into position. Place the sheets on baking trays and leave to dry overnight. The flowers can be made up to a week in advance, and stored when dry in a single layer in an airtight container. (Drying the flowers under a hot lamp – an anglepoise lamp is ideal – will ensure a glossy finish.)

6 To make the white chocolate buttercream, bring a little water to a simmer in a pan then remove from the heat. Put the cream and white chocolate in a heatproof bowl and place over the pan, not touching the water. Stir until smooth then allow to cool slightly.

7 Beat the unsalted butter until light and creamy, then slowly beat in 90g (3oz) icing sugar until the buttercream becomes thick and white. Beat in the cool chocolate mixture.

8 Cut the dome off the cake, if necessary, and then place it upside down on a serving plate or cake board. Spread two-thirds of the white chocolate buttercream over the cake, smoothing it down using a palette knife until the surface is completely covered.

9 Lift the floodwork flowers off the baking paper with a palette knife (ensure that you do this very carefully because they tend to break easily). Gently position the flowers around the top edge of the cake, so they stand up slightly higher than the cake. Arrange the remainder of the flowers in a bunch in the centre.

10 Tint some of the remaining white chocolate buttercream pink and the rest green. Using a paper piping bag, pipe green stems down from the flowers on the side of the cake and from the bunch in the centre.

11 To make pointed leaves, cut the tip of the piping bag into a 'V', press firmly, then pull away. (Practise the leaves first on a piece of greaseproof paper until you are happy with your technique.) Pipe a pink bow in the middle of the bunch of flowers, if liked.

12 The cake will keep for up to three days after decorating, if stored in an airtight container.

With the coloured icing, fill in the centres of the flowers.

The floodwork flowers are fragile so use a palette knife to gently lift them.

Cut a 'V' in the tip of the piping bag to make pointed leaves on the stems.

DECORATING WITH BUTTERCREAM AND MARZIPAN

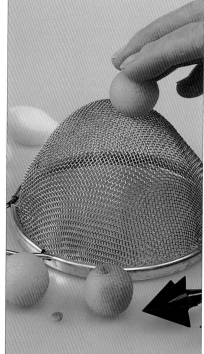

BUTTERCREAM AND MARZIPAN

Buttercream and marzipan are smooth, soft and easy to work with. Buttercream gives a light, delicious coating or filling for a cake and can be piped. Marzipan is an ideal base for royal icing and sugarpaste (rolled fondant), and can be cut and coloured to make decorative shapes, or modelled into fruits, animals and figures (see pages 98–9).

SPREADING A CAKE WITH BUTTERCREAM

Unless the sides of the cake are to be coated, cover the cake completely with buttercream, then swirl the tip of a palette knife over the top and sides to give a decorative finish.

If the cake sides are to be rolled in a coating, such as crushed praline, chocolate vermicelli, grated or chopped chocolate, chopped toasted walnuts, hazelnuts or almonds, coconut or crushed biscuits, spread the sides first with buttercream.

I Use a palette knife to spread roughly. Once covered, run the palette knife around the sides to smooth out the buttercream.

2 Sprinkle the chosen coating on a sheet of greaseproof or non-stick paper. Gently lift the cake, using the palms of your hands to support the top and bottom, and roll it in the coating, gradually turning the cake until the sides are evenly covered.

3 Holding the cake horizontally on one hand, rest the cake board gently over the cake, then flip the cake upright. The top of the cake can now be coated in buttercream.

PIPING BUTTERCREAM

Colour a small amount of buttercream, if liked, and place in a paper bag fitted with an appropriate tube. When piping leaves or blossoms in buttercream, pipe each one onto a small square of greaseproof or non-stick paper.

Shells Use a piping bag fitted with a medium star tube. Holding the bag at an angle of 60° to the surface of the cake, squeeze out the icing, then release the pressure on the bag and pull the tube away to form a tail. Pipe the second shell over the tail (see also page 47).

Leaves Use a piping bag fitted with a leaf tube. Squeeze out a little icing, then as you release the pressure on the bag, pull the tube away to make a point.

Blossoms Use a piping bag fitted with a petal tube. Pipe a tiny petal shape, pulling away the icing at the centre. Pipe four or five more small petals, rotating the paper slightly each time. Using a medium writing tube, pipe a dot of buttercream or sieved jam in the centre of the blossom. Make as many flowers as required (see pages 49, 84–5).

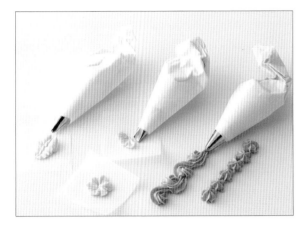

FEATHERING

Feathering makes a simple decoration on any teatime cake.

I   Pipe a border of buttercream around the edge of the cake. Sieve a little jam to remove any pieces, then place in a paper piping bag. Snip off the smallest tip so that the jam flows out in a thin stream.

2   Flood the centre of the cake with glacé icing then, starting at the edge of the cake, pipe a spiral of jam over the glacé icing, gradually working in to the centre.

3   Pull the tip of a cocktail stick (toothpick) or fine skewer through the jam and icing from the centre of the cake towards the edge. Repeat at even intervals all round the cake. Instead of using jam, a different coloured icing is ideal.

MARZIPAN CUTOUTS

This is a simple way of decorating a cake with coloured marzipan cut into a variety of shapes.

I   Tint several pieces of marzipan with food colourings to the required shades. Roll out evenly on an icing sugared surface until about 3mm (⅛in) thick.

2   Using small aspic, cocktail or biscuit (cookie) cutters, cut out shapes. Use small flower and leaf cutters to make a design; cut stems and other leaves from thin strips of marzipan. Arrange the cutout shapes in an attractive design on the cake and secure with apricot glaze or icing.

PATCH

This endearing little pup will appeal to most young children, especially if it bears any resemblance to their favourite family pet.

CAKE AND DECORATION

Madeira cake mixture for 15cm (6in) round tin

1 tbsp cocoa powder, sifted

500g (1lb 2oz) buttercream

60g (2¼oz) sugarpaste (rolled fondant)

black food colouring

3 liquorice 'bootlaces'

15cm (6in) ribbon, about 1cm (½in) wide

1 chocolate gold coin

SPECIAL EQUIPMENT

3.4l (7pt) ovenproof mixing bowl

30cm (12in) round gold or silver cake board

cocktail stick (toothpick)

fine paintbrush

Tip

As only a little sugarpaste is needed for this cake, buy a small packet rather than make your own. It will keep for weeks if tightly wrapped.

1 Preheat the oven to 160°C (325°F/Gas mark 3). Grease and line the base of the mixing bowl. Make up the Madeira cake mixture, turn it into the ovenproof bowl and level the surface. Bake in the oven for about 40 minutes, or until firm. Turn the cake out of the bowl onto a wire rack and leave to cool.

2 Level the surface of the cake by cutting off any peak that formed during baking, so the cake sits flat when inverted onto the cake board. Beat the cocoa powder into a third of the buttercream.

3 Reserve 3 tbsp of the plain buttercream, then spread the remainder over the cake, covering it as smoothly as possible. Spread a little buttercream onto the board at the bottom of the cake and build it up to form a 'neck'. Gently fluff up the surface of the buttercream with the tip of a cocktail stick (toothpick).

4 Spoon the reserved plain buttercream onto the cake in a mound just below the centre, and spread it into a snout shape. Dampen the palette knife, and then smooth down the snout area to contrast with the fluffed-up surface of the rest of the buttercream.

5 Spread a little of the chocolate buttercream over one eye area of the cake. Shape two white eyes from the sugarpaste (rolled fondant) and position on the cake, placing one over the area of the chocolate buttercream.

6 Colour a small piece of sugarpaste black and shape it into an oval nose. Press gently into position on top of the snout.

7 Arrange pieces of liquorice 'bootlace' around the eyes, pressing them gently into the buttercream. Form a smiling mouth from a little more liquorice.

8 Spread small spoonfuls of the chocolate buttercream down each side of the dog's face. Flatten with a palette knife, widening at the base to shape the ears. Fluff up lightly with a cocktail stick. Secure more liquorice around the ears.

9 Paint the centres of the eyes black with food colouring and a fine paintbrush. Arrange the ribbon around the dog's neck, securing the gold coin on it with a dot of buttercream.

Use chocolate buttercream to make ear shapes on either side of the dog's head.

TEDDY GATEAU

Spell out a child's name or a greeting of your choice on the balloons the teddy is holding, to personalize this fun cake.

CAKE AND DECORATION

20cm (8in) Victoria sandwich cake or 2 layers of Genoese

250g (8oz/1 cup) buttercream

few drops vanilla essence (extract)

apricot glaze

75g (3oz/¾ cup) roasted nibbed almonds

75g (3oz) marzipan

selection of food colourings

SPECIAL EQUIPMENT

25cm (10in) round cake board

serrated icing comb

teddy bear template (see page 110)

paper piping bag

no. 2 tube (tip)

1   Fill the cake with buttercream, flavoured with a few drops of vanilla essence, and place on the cake board. Spread the cake with apricot glaze then smooth on a thin layer of buttercream with a palette knife. This will stop any crumbs falling off the cake or mixing with the smooth finish of the buttercream surface. Chill the cake in the refrigerator for about 15 minutes or until the buttercream is firm to the touch.

2   Apply a second coat of buttercream, making it thicker than the first layer. Use a palette knife and a paddling action to layer the cream on. Smooth to a clean finish, ensuring the sides of the gâteau are perpendicular and the top flat.

3   To create a different finish, the top can be textured with a serrated icing comb. Place the cake on a turntable. Hold the comb so that one end is positioned in the centre of the cake and the length of the comb is lightly pressed into the cream across the radius of the cake. Hold the comb in that position with one hand as you turn the cake a full 360° with the other.

4   Press the nibbed nuts onto the side of the cake, brushing away any loose nuts from the board.

5   Colour the marzipan as required by kneading in a little paste colouring. Roll out and cut out the teddy shapes using the template provided on page 110. Add as many balloons as you require for the letters of the name or greeting you wish to spell out. Assemble the shapes on a small board covered with cling film. When firm to the touch, peel the bear and balloons off the cling film and position on the cake.

6   Colour a small amount of buttercream with paste or liquid colouring and pipe the letters of the name or greeting on the balloons with a no.2 tube (tip). Pipe the strings of the balloons in the same way.

Smooth a thin layer of buttercream on the top and sides using a palette knife.

The second coat should be thicker than the first. Smooth the top of the cake flat.

Turn the cake round by 360° while holding a serrated icing comb on top.

Press nibbed nuts or another coating of your choice onto the sides of the cake.

Tip

You could choose other coatings for the sides of the gâteau if you prefer. Chocolate vermicelli, or grated or chopped chocolate would work well, or choose walnuts or hazelnuts in place of almonds.

FESTIVE MARZIPAN WREATH

This Christmas cake is decorated completely with marzipan and a wreath of colourful marzipan fruits, which are simple to make.

CAKE AND DECORATION

20cm (8in) round fruit cake

apricot jam

1.25kg (2½lb) marzipan

white vegetable fat (optional)

dark green, lime green, brown, orange, yellow and red paste food colourings

a little icing (confectioner's) sugar

green and brown dusting powders

edible varnish (optional)

small amount of royal icing

1.5m (5ft) wired-edge organza ribbon (optional)

SPECIAL EQUIPMENT

25cm (10in) round gold cake board

closed curve crimper (PME)

holly cutter (PME)

dimple foam

5-star cone tool (J)

large ball tool (J)

mini star cutter (PME)

1 Place the cake on the board and brush with apricot jam. Roll out 1kg (2¼lb) of the marzipan and use to cover the cake (see page 23). Make sure there are no creases around the base and polish the surface with your hand. Crimp around the base of the cake with a serrated, closed curve crimper. If the crimper sticks, smear on a tiny amount of white vegetable fat.

2 Colour 60g (2¼oz) marzipan dark green and 30g (1¼oz) lime green for the holly leaves. Work in extra icing (confectioner's) sugar until the marzipan is no longer sticky to the touch. Roll out a small amount of each colour, using a non-stick rolling pin. Do not dust with icing sugar. Keep picking up the marzipan as you are rolling out, to prevent it from sticking. Cut out the holly leaves and impress the veins, using a plunger cutter or knife. Twist the leaves slightly and place on dimple foam to prevent them from flattening out. Leave to dry.

3 When the leaves are dry and firm, brush them with dusting powders. As dusting powders dull, you may wish to brush the leaves with a little edible varnish. Allow the leaves to dry completely.

4 Each fruit requires about 10g (¼oz) marzipan. Colour a small amount of marzipan brown for the stalks of the fruits. All the fruits are modelled from the basic ball, pear and sausage shapes described on page 98. Colour the marzipan as required and add texture to appropriate fruits by rolling on a sieve or nutmeg grater. Add stalks, calyxes and leaves as required. The orange stalk and the base of the apple are brown marzipan indented with a modelling tool. The apple and pear stalks are very thinly rolled sausages of brown marzipan. Add extra colour to the fruits by dusting with dusting powder. For a shine, paint with edible varnish.

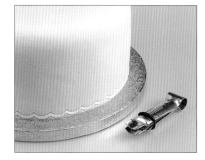

Use a serrated, closed curve crimper to crimp around the base of the cake.

Colour some marzipan dark green and some lime green to make holly leaves.

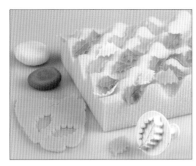

Cut out the holly leaves with a cutter and leave them to dry on dimple foam.

Texture the surface of the oranges and lemons by rolling them on a sieve.

Use a star cone tool to indent a small piece of brown marzipan on the base.

Tip

If preferred, the cake can be covered in sugarpaste of any colour instead of marzipan. For covering with sugarpaste, see page 25.

7 Use 10g (¼oz) natural marzipan to make the peach. Roll into a ball then roll and flatten slightly between the palms of your hands. Indent a line across the top with a blunt blade and make a hole at one end of this line. Colour very lightly with pale yellow, then add a blush of red across the top.

8 Arrange a ring of holly leaves around the top of the cake and place the marzipan fruits in small clusters of two or three, on top of the holly leaves. Secure in place with a little royal icing. Add extra holly leaves between the clusters of fruit. Roll some small balls of red marzipan for berries and attach to the holly. Place an organza ribbon and bow around the cake and attach at the front with royal icing.

DECORATING
WITH CHOCOLATE

CHOCOLATE TECHNIQUES

Chocolate is a versatile and delicious cake decorating medium. It can be simply grated, made into curls or cut-out shapes and piped or drizzled.

WORKING WITH CHOCOLATE

Chocolate has to be melted carefully so that it does not burn. Either use indirect heat, by placing it in a bowl over steaming water, or use a microwave.

By indirect heat

1 Chop the chocolate into pieces and put in a heatproof bowl. Bring a pan of water to the boil and remove from heat.
2 Sit the bowl over the pan, making sure the base of the bowl is not sitting in the water. Stir occasionally, until the chocolate has melted. Take care not to let any water into the chocolate or it will 'sieze' and form a hard mass.

Using a microwave

Place the chocolate in a microwave-safe bowl and microwave on High in 30-second bursts, testing by stirring each time, until melted. Microwaved chocolate will hold its shape when soft so don't be deceived – you will need to stir it to check if it has melted or not.

COVERING A CAKE WITH CHOCOLATE

Place the cake on a wire rack over a large plate. Melt dark, milk or white chocolate, or make ganache (see page 75) and leave to thicken slightly. Pour the chocolate onto the top of the cake and allow it to run out to the edges. Ease it around the sides using a palette knife until the cake is completely covered.

DRIZZLING CHOCOLATE

This makes a simple and attractive decoration for cakes covered with melted chocolate or ganache (see page 75).

1 Put some melted chocolate (in a contrasting flavour to that used on the cake) in a paper piping bag and snip off the smallest tip so the chocolate flows out in a fine stream.
2 Holding the piping bag 5cm (2in) above the cake, pipe lines by gently squeezing the bag, moving your hand quickly over the cake.
3 Tilt the cake slightly to cover the sides as well as the top.

Drizzle a white chocolate pattern on top of milk or dark chocolate for an attractive and unusual finish.

CARAQUE OR CURLS

1 Melt 250g (8¾oz) dark or white chocolate in a heat-proof bowl set over a pan of simmering water, and pour onto a marble slab or other surface. Spread thinly and leave to set.

2 Draw the blade of a large knife, held at an angle of 45°, across the surface of the chocolate to remove a thin layer that rolls into curls. Transfer the curls to a large plate as you make them.

3 Chill the caraque or keep it in a cool place until you are ready to use it.

For double chocolate caraque, use 125g (4oz) each of dark and white chocolate. Melt in separate heatproof bowls over saucepans of gently simmering water. Spread the dark chocolate over the slab, then swirl with the white. Leave to set then make caraque as above.

CHOCOLATE ROLLS

Pour melted chocolate onto a work surface or marble slab, and spread thinly with a palette knife. Leave until barely set. Cut the chocolate to the width of a clean paint scraper, then place the scraper at an angle of 45° to the chocolate. Push the scraper forwards, encouraging the chocolate to curl in front of the scraper. Trim the rolls with a hot knife.

CUT-OUTS

There are many different cutters available commercially, from animals and flowers to geometric shapes.

1 Pour melted dark or white chocolate onto a sheet of greaseproof or non-stick paper. Spread out the chocolate with a palette knife.

2 Lift the paper at the edges and shake gently so that the chocolate spreads into a thin, even layer. Encourage the palette knife lines to disappear.

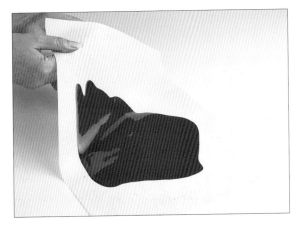

3 Leave until just set. Using cutters, press out shapes and lift away from the paper with a knife or spatula. Or to cut out other shapes, use a sharp knife with a rocking action for straight lines or the tip of a sharp knife for curves.

4 Chill until ready to use. When the shapes are firmly set, ease them away from the greaseproof paper by sliding a knife underneath.

5 Lift them into the finished position by lightly holding the side of the shapes so that no fingermarks are left on the chocolate surface.

IRREGULAR SHAPES

Spread rows of melted chocolate about 10cm (4in) wide over wrinkled cling film, using a palette knife. Leave to set. Break into pieces and use to decorate the sides of a cake (see Continental Wedding Cake on page 76).

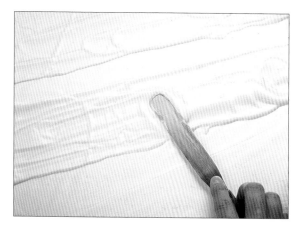

CHOCOLATE PIPING

1 To give greater control of melted chocolate for piping designs, carefully stir in a few drops of glycerine. Allow time for the chocolate to react with the glycerine to create the new consistency. This could take a few seconds.

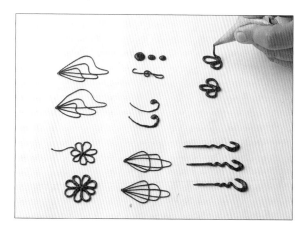

2 Place the piping chocolate in a small greaseproof piping bag and cut a small hole (approximately the size of a no.1 tube/tip) in its point. Pipe the required designs onto a sheet of greaseproof paper and leave to set. Chill if necessary.

3 Ease each piece away from the paper using a palette knife, then slide the decoration into position.

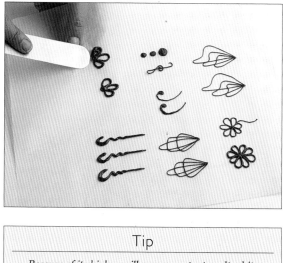

Tip

Because of its higher milk-sugar content, melt white chocolate in a bowl over hot water to prevent burning.

CHOCOLATE LEAVES

Gently wipe leaves with a damp cloth. Melt a little dark, milk or white chocolate and, using a paintbrush, brush it thickly on the underside of each leaf. Chill until set, then peel the leaves away from the chocolate.

GRATED CHOCOLATE

Different textures of chocolate can be created by using a simple grater. Use large blocks of chocolate, discarding the small ends which can be used for melting.

Fine shred This is achieved using the small blades on the grater; use for smaller cakes or coating the side of a gâteau as an alternative to chocolate vermicelli.

Large shred A heavier shred gives the chocolate the appearance of small curls for use on larger gâteaux.

GANACHE

150ml (4½fl oz/⅔ cup) whipping cream
225g (8oz) plain chocolate, broken into small pieces

Ganache is a rich mixture of cream and chocolate. It can be used in many ways: whipped as a filling or coating, or warmed for a pour-over coating.

1   Put the cream in a pan and heat gently until boiling. Remove from the heat and pour over the chocolate. Stir until the chocolate has melted and has blended into a rich dark mixture. Pour into a clean bowl.

2   Allow the ganache to set. To pour over a cake, bring the set ganache to pouring consistency by warming gently. For piping and filling on cakes, whip until light, fluffy and pale.

CONTINENTAL WEDDING CAKE

For a truly spectacular wedding cake that is a little out of the ordinary,
try this white chocolate continental dream.

CAKE AND DECORATION

18cm (7in) and 25cm (10in) genoese cakes

185ml (6fl oz) Cointreau

300g (11oz) white chocolate drops, melted

165g (5½ oz) sugar

cream ribbon

FOR THE WHITE GANACHE

150g (5oz) white chocolate drops

135g (4½oz) white chocolate

125ml (4fl oz) cream

250g (8oz) unsalted butter

FOR THE CUSTARD

75g (2¾oz) cornflour (cornstarch)

60g (2¼oz) custard powder

150g (5oz) caster (superfine) sugar

2 tsp vanilla essence (extract)

375ml (12fl oz) cream

500ml (16fl oz) milk

2 egg yolks

1   To make the white ganache, put all the ingredients in a pan and stir over low heat until smooth. Transfer to a bowl, cover with cling film and leave until cold (don't refrigerate). Beat for 3–5 minutes, or until light and fluffy.

2   To make the custard filling, put the cornflour (cornstarch), custard, sugar and vanilla in a pan. Gradually add the cream and milk, whisking until free of lumps. Stir over low heat until it comes to the boil. Reduce the heat and simmer for 3 minutes. Remove from the heat and quickly stir in the egg yolks. Transfer to a bowl, cover with cling film and refrigerate for 30 minutes, stirring occasionally.

3   Slice each cake horizontally into three layers. Put the bottom layer of the large cake on a plate. Brush with Cointreau and spread with a third of the custard. Top with another layer of cake, Cointreau and custard. Brush the underside of the top layer with Cointreau and place on top. Cover with two thirds of the ganache.

4   Place the bottom layer of the small cake on top of the larger cake. Brush with Cointreau and spread with half the remaining custard. Top with the next layer, brush with Cointreau and spread with custard. Brush the underside of the top layer with Cointreau and place on top. Cover with the remaining ganache and chill.

5   Lay out two sheets of cling film. Wrinkle the surface and spread with two rows of chocolate about 10cm (4in) high. Leave to set (see page 74). Break into pieces. Place around the cakes, overlapping the pieces slightly.

6   Cover three baking trays with foil. Place a pan over medium heat and sprinkle with sugar – as it melts, add the rest gradually. Stir to melt any lumps and prevent burning. When golden brown, remove from heat. Drizzle the melted sugar on the trays, cool, then peel away the foil. Tie ribbon around cake and top with toffee pieces.

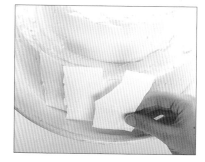

Break the chocolate into pieces and arrange, overlapping, around the cake.

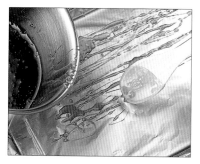

Once the toffee is a dark, caramel colour, drizzle over the foil-covered trays.

CHOCOLATE LEAF CAKE

*Collect fresh rose leaves from the garden to make the
markings on your chocolate leaves totally authentic.*

CAKE AND DECORATION

double quantity ganache
(see page 75)

20cm (8in) round chocolate
cake

100g (4oz) plain chocolate,
broken into pieces

SPECIAL EQUIPMENT

25cm (10in) round cake
board or plate

piping bag

no. 13 piping tube (tip)

fresh rose leaves

small paintbrush

1   Place some set ganache in the bowl of an electric mixer and whisk with a balloon whisk until light, fluffy and paler. Use to fill and thinly coat the cake. Chill in the refrigerator.

2   Warm some set ganache in a bowl over hot water or on a low setting in the microwave. Place the chilled, coated cake on a wire rack. Pour the ganache over the cake and spread with a palette knife, making sure the sides are coated. Lift the cake off the wire rack with a palette knife and place in position on the cake board or plate. Leave to set in the refrigerator.

3   Place some whisked ganache in a piping bag fitted with a no. 13 piping tube (tip) and pipe a shell border around the base of the cake (see page 47).

4   Place the small pieces of plain chocolate in a bowl and set over a pan of water that has just boiled. Stir occasionally until the chocolate has melted, taking care not to splash any water into the bowl.

5   You will need approximately 23 rose leaves for this design (or use another kind of leaf with clear markings if you wish). Gently wipe them clean with a damp cloth, being careful not to tear them. Using a paintbrush, paint the underside of the leaves with a thick coating of melted chocolate. For a contrast, you can use different coloured chocolate to make the leaves, if you wish.

6   Leave to set in the refrigerator. A second coat of melted chocolate may be necessary. Once they have set, carefully peel the leaves away from the chocolate, revealing the markings.

7   Arrange the chocolate leaves directly on top of the cake, in a pattern of your choosing. Here, we have displayed the leaves by laying them in a circle overlapping each other.

Tip.

Ganache should be at room temperature before whisking. If it starts to curdle (possibly because the mixture was too cool), add a knob of butter and whisk again.

*Pour the whisked ganache over the cake
and spread it with a palette knife.*

*Pipe a neat shell border of whisked
ganache round the base of the cake.*

CHOCOLATE CHERRY GATEAU

A perennial favourite, similar to Black Forest Cake, this is a chocaholic's dream. Maraschino cherries are dipped in white chocolate to decorate.

CAKE AND DECORATION

4-egg chocolate-flavoured Genoese mixture (see page 13)

1 quantity chocolate ganache (see page 75)

60g (2oz) white chocolate

3 maraschino cherries

125g (4oz) dark chocolate

250g (8oz) whole fruit morello cherry jam

2 tbsp lemon juice

2 tbsp maraschino syrup

SPECIAL EQUIPMENT

two 20cm (8in) round cake tins (pans)

3 small rose leaves

Tip

Fresh fruits dipped in melted chocolate make delicious cake decorations, especially strawberries.

1 Preheat the oven to 180°C (350°F/Gas mark 4). Bake the sponges in the lined and greased cake tins (pans) then cool them on a wire rack. For the chocolate flavour, replace 1½tbsp flour with 1½tbsp sifted cocoa powder.

2 Make up the ganache mixture and refrigerate for an hour before whisking.

3 Melt the dark chocolate and spread it over a marble or smooth surface. Leave to dry then follow the instructions on page 73 to make the chocolate caraque. Rolls are made in the same way as caraque, but using a clean paint scraper.

4 Melt the white chocolate. Drain the maraschino cherries on absorbent kitchen paper. Half dip them in warm chocolate then leave them to dry on wax paper. Wash and dry the rose leaves, then brush the backs with white chocolate. Refrigerate chocolate-side-up until set, then very carefully peel the leaves off the chocolate. Make extras in case of breakages.

5 Warm the jam, lemon juice and maraschino syrup in a pan until the jam has softened. Brush liberally over both sponge layers to cover, then spoon out the cherries remaining in the pan and spread them over one of the cakes.

6 Whisk the ganache until pale and doubled in volume. Spread one third of it over the cherries. Place the second sponge on top, jam side down. Spread the remaining ganache over the cake and smooth over with a palette knife.

7 Press the chocolate caraque around the side of the cake and arrange half-dipped cherries and leaves on top. Chill the cake before serving.

Cut out the chocolate scrolls to decorate the sides of the cake.

Use real leaves to make the white chocolate decorations.

DECORATING WITH
SUGAR FLOWERS

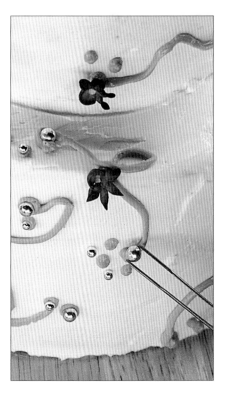

FLOWER TECHNIQUES

Making sugar flowers is an absorbing aspect of sugarcraft. There are many different techniques for making flowers, from moulding through to using cutters, and you can use sugarpaste (rolled fondant) or flower paste (gum paste). (For royal icing flowers, see pages 48–9.) Combine them with sugar foliage and ribbon loops to make attractive cake decorations.

MOULDED ROSES

1 Knead colouring into the flower paste (gum paste) until it is the colour you require. (Alternatively, roses can be shaped in white and then highlighted with dusting powder and a fine paintbrush.)

2 Take a piece of paste about the size of a grape and shape it into a cone. Pinch the cone around the centre to form a 'waist'.

3 Take another small ball of paste and press it between your fingers and thumbs to shape it into a petal. Wrap this around the cone.

4 Shape another slightly larger petal and wrap this around the cone, overlapping the first petal. Continue building up the rose, making each petal slightly larger than the one before.

5 Open out, and roll the tips of the outer petals outwards slightly to create a realistic shape. Once completed, slice off the rose through its base and use the base to shape the next cone. Leave overnight to harden.

BLOSSOMS

For simple yet pretty decorative flowers, and to save time and effort, use a 'plunger' blossom cutter (see page 8).

1 Knead colouring into the sugarpaste or flower paste until it is the colour you require. Roll out the paste as thinly as possible on a surface dusted with icing (confectioner's) sugar.

2 Dip the cutter into icing sugar, then press out a blossom shape. Push the shape out of the cutter onto a piece of foam to create a curved blossom.

3 Push a pin through the centre if attaching a stamen. Leave overnight to harden. Thread stamens through.

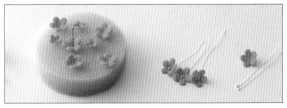

PETUNIAS

Petunias come in shades of pink, purple and white, so choose those colours of flower paste for a realistic effect.

1 Take a small piece of flower paste, about the size of a large pea, and shape it into a cone. Place the cone flat end

down on a surface dusted with icing sugar and, using a small rolling pin or the handle of paintbrush, roll out the edges as thinly as possible.

2   Cut out the flower using a small or large petunia cutter (available from cake decoration suppliers). Mark each petal by pressing with a flower veiner.

3   Press a ball modelling tool into the middle of the flower to shape the centre. Roll the edges of each petal with a cocktail stick (toothpick) to frill slightly. Leave overnight.

4   To add colour, either immediately or after hardening, lightly dust each petunia petal with colouring powder, using a fine paintbrush.

5   Put a little royal icing in a paper piping bag, snip off a small tip, and pipe a dot into the centre of each petunia. Press several small stamens into the icing to secure.

Note There are hundreds of types of flower cutters available, all of which should be used as described here.

3   Simply mark veins in the leaf using a sharp knife. Alternatively, vein the leaf in a leaf veiner, then remove the leaf and pinch the back of the centre vein to give greater definition. Colour the leaves with dusting powder, as required.

LEAVES

Once mastered, the basic technique for leaves can be applied to nearly any kind of leaf.

1   Roll out some green flower paste, angling the rolling pin slightly to create a wedge of thicker paste. (Alternatively, use a grooved board or rolling pin, manufactured for this purpose.) Cut out a leaf using a cutter, positioning it so that the ridge of thicker paste is at the base of the leaf.

2   Soften the edge of the leaf with a dogbone tool on the palm of your hand or a pad of hard foam.

DAISY CAKE

Small, foil-wrapped chocolate eggs, half-hidden under clusters of moulded flowers, make a pretty decoration for a Springtime celebration cake.

CAKE AND DECORATION

23cm (9in) plain or flavoured Madeira cake (see page 12)

60g (2oz) flower paste (gum paste)

icing (confectioner's) sugar for dusting

1.5kg (3¼lb) sugarpaste (rolled fondant)

yellow food colouring

45ml (3tbsp) apricot glaze

1kg (2¼lb) marzipan

10–12 mini chocolate eggs

gold foil

15ml (1 tbsp) icing sugar

1m (3ft) purple ribbon, approx 5cm (2in) wide

SPECIAL EQUIPMENT

small and large daisy or simple flower cutters

a small square of tulle

fine paintbrush

30cm (12in) round gold or silver cake board

1 To make the daisies, roll out the flower paste (gum paste) as thinly as possible on a surface dusted with icing (confectioner's) sugar. Cut out shapes with daisy or flower cutters. You will need 8 large flowers and 24 small. Cup the flowers slightly between your fingers, then place on a piece of crumpled foil and leave to harden for several hours. The crumpled foil allows the cut-out daisies to harden in a 'cupped' shape.

2 Colour 60g (2oz) of the sugarpaste (rolled fondant) deep yellow. Roll a small piece into a ball and press it against a piece of tulle until the netting leaves a realistic textured impression in the icing. Pull away the tulle. Using a fine paintbrush and a little water, lightly dampen the centre of the flower, then position the yellow ball in it. Repeat with the remainder.

3 Brush the cake with apricot glaze and cover with marzipan. Place on the board. Reserve 125g (4oz) of the remaining white sugarpaste and colour the rest pale yellow. Use to cover the cake.

4 Use the remaining white sugarpaste to cover the cake board around the cake. Use the remaining deep yellow sugarpaste to make a 'twist' border around the base of the cake. For this, thinly roll out the sugarpaste. Cut out a 5mm (¼ in) wide strip and lightly twist it from the ends. Lay the strip gently around the base of the cake.

5 Wrap the eggs in gold foil. Gold foil is most readily available on bought chocolate bars. Using a dampened paintbrush, secure the daisies and eggs to the cake. To secure the ribbon, make a paste with icing (confectioner's) sugar and a dash of water. Wrap the ribbon around the cake and secure the ends with a dot of paste.

Place the flowers on some crumpled foil to dry and shape.

Use a piece of netting to make the pattern in the flower centres.

PETUNIA WEDDING CAKE

This pretty cake, decorated with simple flowers and frills, can be successfully tackled by any inexperienced but keen cake decorator.

CAKE AND DECORATION

28cm (11in) and 15cm (6in) hexagonal rich fruit cakes

6 tbsp apricot glaze

2kg (4¼lb) marzipan

icing (confectioner's) sugar for dusting

2.5kg (5½lb) sugarpaste (rolled fondant)

pink and leaf green food colourings

2.5m (8ft) fine white ribbon

125g (4¼oz) flower paste (gum paste)

pink and green food dusting powders

250g (9oz) royal icing

white stamens

1m (3ft) white ribbon, about 5mm (¼in) wide

1m (3ft) pink ribbon, about 5mm (¼in) wide

white floristry wire

sprigs of ivy (optional)

For Special Equipment, see page 90

1 Brush the cakes with apricot glaze and cover with marzipan, allowing 500g (1lb 2oz) for the smaller cake and 1.5kg (3¼lb) for the large. Place the cakes on the cake boards.

2 Reserve 500g (1lb 2oz) of the sugarpaste (rolled fondant) for decoration. Use the remainder to cover the cakes, allowing 500g (1lb 2oz) for the small cake and 1.5kg (3¼lb) for the large. Reserve the trimmings.

3 Halve the reserved 500g (1lb 2oz) sugarpaste. Mix one half with the trimmings and colour very pale pink. Colour the other half green. Use some of the pink sugarpaste to cover the cake boards around the base of the cakes.

4 Trace the templates on page 108 onto greaseproof or non-stick paper. Cut them out. Place the large template against one side of the large cake. Mark the curved outline onto the cake using a pin. Repeat on all sides then use the small template to mark outlines on the small cake.

5 Position fine white ribbon around the base of each cake, securing with a dampened paintbrush.

6 To make the the bottom layer of frills, use green sugarpaste and a frill cutter (see page 31). Secure the frills on the sides of the cake with water and a fine paintbrush, so that the top edge of each frill comes 5mm (¼in) below the template line.

7 Using the pink sugarpaste, shape one piece of frill and position it above the green frill so that the top edge just covers the template line. Smooth the top edge lightly with your finger, then use a scalloped crimper to make a decorative edge (see page 32). Repeat, adding pink frills to all sides of the cake.

Place the template against the cake and mark the curved outline with a pin.

Crimp the edges of the frills around the sides using a scalloped crimper.

SPECIAL EQUIPMENT

38cm (15in) hexagonal or round silver cake board

23cm (9in) hexagonal or round silver cake board

templates (see page 108)

frill cutter

scalloped crimping tool

small and large petunia cutters

leaf veiner

ball modelling tool

cocktail stick (toothpick)

paper piping bag

large writing tube (tip)

3 hollow cake pillars, about 7.5–8.5cm (3–3½in) high

3 dowel rods, about 23cm (9in) long

8 To make the petunias, colour half the flower paste (gum paste) pale pink and leave the rest white. Take a piece about the size of a large pea and shape it into a cone. Place the cone, flat end down, on a surface dusted with icing sugar and, using the handle of a paintbrush or small rolling pin, roll out the edges thinly. Cut out a flower using a small or large petunia cutter. Mark each petal by pressing with a leaf veiner. Press a ball modelling tool into the middle of the flower to shape the centre. Roll the edges of each petal with a cocktail stick to frill slightly. Make a selection of flowers from pink and white paste (see pages 84–5), then leave overnight.

9 To colour the flowers, dust each petal with pink and green dusting powder, using a fine paintbrush. Put a little royal icing in a paper piping bag, snip off a small tip, and pipe a dot into the centre of each petunia. Press several small stamens into the icing to secure.

10 To make wired ribbon, cut a 6cm (2½in) length of floristry wire and a 10cm (4in) length of fine ribbon. Fold the ribbon in half so the ends meet. Wrap the wire round the centre of the folded ribbon, then twist the ends of the wire tightly. Snip off the wire and secure the ribbons to the cake with icing. Use pink and white ribbons to make about 8 ribbon sprays in each colour.

11 Position the cake pillars equally spaced in a triangle about 12cm (4½in) apart on the larger cake. Push a stick of dowelling down the centre of each pillar and right through to the base of the cake, making sure you keep the dowelling vertical. Using a pencil, mark the dowelling at a point level with the tops of the pillars. Remove the sticks and saw off the excess. Reposition the sticks and check that the top tier sits comfortably over the pillars.

12 To assemble the decorations, roughly position the petunias between the pillars and top edges of the bottom tier and in a small cluster on the top tier. Alternate the colours and make sure that each flower faces outwards. Using a little royal icing and a paper piping bag fitted with a large writing tube (tip), secure each flower in position. Use the ribbon sprays to fill any gaps between the flowers, securing them with icing onto the cakes. Before assembling the tiers, tuck ivy sprigs, if using, in among the flowers and ribbons.

Wired ribbons are used to enhance small clusters of flowers.

If the dowel rods are higher than the pillars, saw them until they are level.

VIOLET DREAM

This elegant cake is a show-stopper at just about any occasion. Cream and purple were chosen for a sophisticated colour scheme, but you can colour the icing any shade you like.

1   To make meringue frosting to coat the cakes, put the egg whites and sugar in a heatproof bowl. Bring a small pan of water to a simmer and place the bowl over the pan (don't let the base of the bowl touch the water). Stir continuously to dissolve the sugar, but be careful not to cook the egg whites.

2   When the sugar has dissolved, remove from the heat and beat the mixture with electric beaters for 5 minutes, or until stiff peaks form. Cut the butter into about 10 pieces and add, piece by piece, beating after each addition. The mixture should thicken when you have about 2 pieces of butter left, but continue until you have added all the butter.

3   Using a sharp serrated knife, trim the domed top from each cake to give a level surface. Place a large cake upside down on a plate, so that the flat base becomes the top. Spread some of the frosting evenly over the top and side of the cake with a palette or flat-bladed knife.

4   Sandwich with the other large cake, then spread frosting over the top and side. Put the small cake on top. Reserve about 3 tbsp of the frosting and spread the remainder smoothly over the top cake.

5   Add a few drops of food colouring to the reserved frosting to tint it a pale colour (we used purple) and spoon into a small paper piping bag. Pipe squiggles over the top and side of the cake.

6   You will need about 25 sugar violets. To make them, colour the flower paste (gum paste) with violet food colouring. Take a small ball of paste, roll smooth and model it into a teardrop. Dip the pointed end of a dowel rod into white fat (shortening) and rub into the wood. Push the pointed end of the dowel into the

CAKE AND DECORATION

4 egg whites
220g (7¾oz/1 cup) caster (superfine) sugar
330g (11½oz/1½ cups) unsalted butter
two 20cm (8in) and one 15cm (6in) round cakes (carrot or chocolate)
25cm (10in) cake board or cake platter
purple, violet, black and yellow paste food colourings
silver dragees
115g (4oz) flower paste (gum paste)
yellow dusting powder (blossom dust)
clear alcohol (gin or vodka)

Beat until stiff peaks form, then beat in the butter piece by piece.

Place the small cake on top of the other two iced cakes.

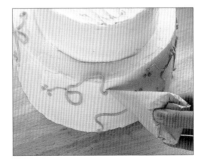

Pipe wavy lines all over the cake using purple icing.

SPECIAL EQUIPMENT

pointed dowel rod

fine paintbrush

large end of the teardrop then remove and, using scissors, cut two small (at the top), two medium (one each side) and one large petal (at the bottom) in the opened end of the teardrop.

7   Pinch and flatten each petal, easing the top pair and the bottom one backwards slightly, and tweaking the two side petals inwards and upwards. Allow the flowers to dry and harden overnight.

8   Dust the centre of the flowers with yellow dusting powder and then paint lines with a fine brush and black food colouring mixed with alcohol. Alternatively, colour a little flower paste yellow, roll into tiny balls and place one in the centre of each violet.

9   Use a pair of tweezers to decorate the cake with the dragees and sugar violets.

10   This cake can be decorated up to 2 days in advance. Keep the two halves separately in airtight containers in the refrigerator (unless you have an enormous container that will hold the whole cake). Reassemble and return to room temperature before serving.

Making violets

Although flower decorations can be bought, these simple violets are easy to make and are the perfect finishing touch.

Push the pointed end of the dowel into the large end of the teardrop shape.

Using scissors cut two small, two medium and one large petal.

Pinch and flatten each petal easing the top pair and bottom one backwards.

Paint lines with a fine paintbrush or leave the violets plain.

Tip

Make this cake with tiny red roses, pretty pink blossoms or any other small flowers of your choice.

CHRISTMAS ROSE CAKE

A ring of Christmas roses and rich collar of festive ribbon transforms a simple
royal-iced cake into something special.

CAKE AND DECORATION

20cm (8in) round rich or light fruit cake

3 tbsp apricot glaze

1kg (2¼lb) marzipan

125g (4¼oz) sugarpaste (rolled fondant)

675g (1½lb) royal icing (optional)

50g (2oz) flower paste (gum paste)

yellow dusting powder

white stamens

75cm (30in) firm gold ribbon, about 5cm (2½in) wide

2m (2yd) fine green or red wired ribbon

1m (3ft) fine ribbon for board edge

SPECIAL EQUIPMENT

28cm (11in) round gold cake board

medium rose petal cutter

cocktail sticks (toothpicks)

piece of foam sponge

soft paintbrush

paper piping bag

1   Brush the cake with apricot glaze and cover with marzipan. Place on the cake board. Cover the edges of the board with sugarpaste (rolled fondant) if liked. Reserve 4 tablespoons of the royal icing. Spread the remainder over the top and sides of the cake until covered in one even layer. Work the palette knife around the side of the cake, then over the top to neaten. Leave to set.

2   To make the Christmas roses, roll some strips of foil, then shape into rounds about 5cm (2in) in diameter. Place on a sheet of greaseproof paper. You will need 11 altogether, allowing one spare. Take a little flower paste (gum paste) and roll as thinly as possible. Cut out five petals with the cutter. Roll a cocktail stick over the edges of the petal to give a delicate, lightly curled edge. Press each petal onto a piece of sponge to lightly cup it.

3   Lightly dampen one side of each of the five petals. Arrange the petals, slightly overlapping, inside a foil ring so that the rose is supported by the foil. Make the remaining roses in the same way and leave to harden for 24 hours.

4   Using the soft brush, lightly colour the centre of each rose with dusting powder. Place the reserved royal icing in the piping bag and snip off the tip. Pipe a dot of icing into the centre of a rose. Cut about a dozen stamens down to 1cm (½in) depth and press several at a time into the royal icing. Finish the remainder in the same way.

5   Secure the roses in a ring around the edge of the cake with a dot of royal icing. Tie the firm gold ribbon around the cake and secure with a little icing. Loosely pleat the wired ribbon concertina-fashion between the fingers and thumbs. Secure over the gold ribbon. Secure the fine ribbon around the edge of the board.

Cover the cake with royal icing and create a pattern with a palette knife.

Cut out 5 petals for each flower, lightly frill the edges and rest them on sponge.

MODELLING ON CAKES

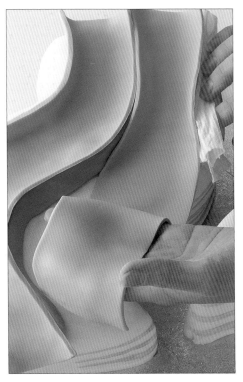

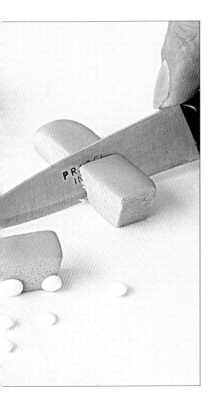

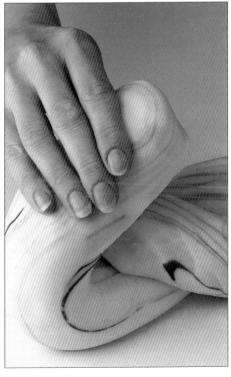

MODELLING TECHNIQUES

There are several mediums suitable for modelling – sugarpaste (rolled fondant), modelling paste and marzipan are the main ones. Here are instructions for some basic figures that you can adapt as you wish.

BASIC SHAPES

All modelling starts with a ball. As well as being a shape in itself, the process of rolling a ball will ensure a perfectly smooth surface from which to model everything else.

To make a ball, knead the paste lightly, place it in the palms of your hands and rotate. Keep your fingers well stretched out to polish the paste smooth as it rolls around.

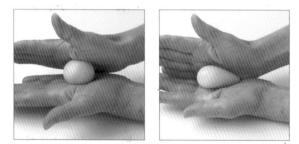

For a pear shape, open the palms of your hands and rock them backwards and forwards. Pressure from the sides of your hands will thin one side, while the thicker side protrudes between your thumbs.

For a sausage shape, start by rolling a ball. Although a sausage can be modelled in your hands, for a bump-free, perfectly smooth finish, use a sugarpaste smoother and roll the paste backwards and forwards on a hard surface or non-stick board.

FIGURES

When using several figures on a cake, they need to be small enough not to overwhelm the rest of the cake. A 30g (1¼oz) piece of modelling paste will make a body about 5cm (2in) long (not including the head). You will need very little equipment to start with; just modelling paste (see page 19), a few cocktail sticks (toothpicks) and drinking straws for marking features. Vegetable fat on your fingers will help you achieve a smooth finish and prevent sticking. Assemble the pieces after drying or while still soft with water, icing or sugar glue. Paint on features and details when the figures are dry. See pages 102 and 106 for simple figure modelling.

1   Roll a ball of modelling paste into a sausage shape, slightly thicker at one end. Pinch out the paste on either side of the thick end to make arms, rolling between your finger and thumb to lengthen.

2   Level the base of the body and make a hem. Open the sleeves and make a neck hole. Make legs or trousers by cutting up the centre of the base and open the trouser bottoms with a skewer to make shoes.

3   To make a head, roll flesh-coloured modelling paste into a smooth ball. Put it in the palm of one hand and roll the other index finger lightly over the centre to make a fat

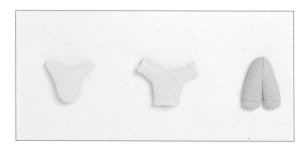

peanut shape. Pinch the paste at the lower back of the head to make a neck. You can insert a piece of uncooked spaghetti into the neck for extra strength. Mark eyes, eyebrows and mouth with the end of a drinking straw.

4 Attach a small cone of paste to either side of the head for ears. Press the narrow end into the head with a paintbrush handle to hollow out the ear. Make noses with balls or cones. Mark nostrils with a pin after attaching.

5 Make different hairstyles by texturing rolled-out paste – a curved blade modelling tool is useful. Use round or daisy cutters to cut out hair; shred the edge and lay over the head.

6 Allow heads to dry before painting. Use well-diluted paste colours and a very fine paintbrush. To give a blush to cheeks, use plum dusting powder mixed with cornflour.

7 To make feet, roll a cone and pinch one end to flatten. Nails can be marked with a thin drinking straw cut to the shape of a nail. Mark the end of the foot and cut with a scalpel to separate the toes. For hands, make a flattened cone of flesh-coloured paste, with a narrow end for the wrist. Cut a 'V' from one side for the thumb, then make three cuts for fingers. Mark the nails with a straw.

TEDDY BEAR

1 Roll two balls of icing, one slightly smaller than the other. Gently press the small one on top of the larger one.

2 Shape two flattened rounds of paste. Halve one and position for the ears; position the other for a muzzle.

3 Shape the arms and legs and secure to the body. Use a contrasting colour to make the paw pads and the centres of the ears.

4 To complete the teddy, paint faint features on the head using a fine paintbrush and diluted colouring.

DUCK

1 Make a sausage of white paste, tapered to thin at both ends. Tweak one end upwards and thin out to make a tail. Elongate the other end and mould into a head and neck.

2 Make indents for eyes. Make a point at the front of the head where the beak will be painted. Roll a piece of paste thinly and cut out wings, freehand or using a template. Texture with feathers, using a tool or the end of a drinking straw.

3 Roll tiny black balls for eyes. Roll out orange paste and cut into webbed feet. Attach the wings and feet to the body. Press the eyes in place. Paint on the beak when dry.

PIG

1 Shape a large sausage into a body and make indents where the head and legs will be. Make small trotters from ovals with one end flattened and a cut made for the trotters.

2 Make the head from another oval, elongated at one end to form a snout. Bend the snout up slightly and make two holes for the nose and a line for the mouth.

3 Make indents and insert small balls of black paste for the eyes. Make ears from circles of paste, cupped with a ball tool. Paint on colouring when dry.

Use coloured modelling paste, or paint or dust these animals when dry. Experiment to make other animals in the same way.

CHRISTENING CAKE

This very pretty christening cake would look equally effective coloured pale blue or yellow.

CAKE AND DECORATION

2kg (4½lb) sugarpaste (rolled fondant)

pink food colouring

23cm (9in) and 15cm (6in) round rich fruit cakes

5 tbsp apricot glaze

1.5kg (3¼lb) marzipan

icing (confectioner's) sugar for dusting

SPECIAL EQUIPMENT

30cm (12in) round silver cake board

15cm (6in) round cake card

large and fine paintbrushes

templates on page 108

1   Reserve 185g (6½oz) white sugarpaste (rolled fondant). Colour 60g (2¼oz) of the remainder bright pink. Colour another 185g (6½oz) a paler shade of pink. Colour the remaining sugarpaste a very pale pink, adding the colouring very cautiously.

2   Brush the cakes with apricot glaze and cover with marzipan (see page 23), allowing 500g (1lb 2oz) for the small cake and 1kg (2¼lb) for the large cake. Place the large cake on the cake board.

3   Reserve 60g (2oz) of the palest pink icing. Use the remainder to cover the cake, allowing 500g (1lb 2oz) for the small cake and 1kg (2¼lb) for the large cake. When covering the small cake, stand it on a cake card covered with a sheet of greaseproof or non-stick paper.

4   Using a spatula, lift and position the small cake slightly to one side of the larger one. Use a little white sugarpaste to cover the cake board around the base of the large cake (see page 27). Use more of the white and palest pink sugarpaste to make a sugarpaste rope around the base of each cake (see page 33).

5   Use the different shades of pink and white sugarpaste to make the decorations. See page 99 for instructions on how to make the teddies.

6   To make building blocks, simply mould neat cubes of sugarpaste.

7   For the train, shape and position the engine and carriages, and then add tiny white wheels. For the train 'steam', use thinly rolled white sugarpaste cut to shape using the templates on page 108.

8   Arrange the decorations on the cake while still soft, securing with a dampened paintbrush. Alternatively, leave them to harden and then secure, using a paste made from a little icing sugar and water.

Follow the instructions on page 99 to make the teddies from sugarpaste.

Cut out the railway engine and carriages then add tiny white wheels.

CHRISTMAS NATIVITY

The design of this cake is effective in its simplicity. Both the stable and figures are exceptionally easy to shape.

CAKE AND DECORATION

25cm (10in) square rich or light fruit cake

4 tbsp apricot glaze

1.25kg (2¾lb) marzipan

icing (confectioner's) sugar for dusting

2.5kg (5lb) sugarpaste (rolled fondant)

brown, purple, red, black, dark and light blue, green and yellow food colourings

125g (4¼oz) icing (confectioner's) sugar

1.5m (5ft) cream cord

2m (6½ft) ribbon

SPECIAL EQUIPMENT

30cm (12in) square silver cake board

templates, see page 109

small star cutter

4 and 5cm (1½ and 2in) round cutters

cocktail stick (toothpick)

paper piping bag

fine paintbrush

1   Brush the cake with apricot glaze and cover with marzipan. Place on the cake board. Colour 250g (9oz) of the sugarpaste (rolled fondant) dark brown. Alternatively, use pastillage (see page 22).

2   Trace and cut out the stable templates on page 109 onto non-stick or greaseproof paper. Thinly roll the brown sugarpaste and lay on a sheet of non-stick paper. Lay the templates over the sugarpaste and cut around them, then carefully peel away the excess paste. (You will need two roof templates and two side templates.)

3   Roll and cut out a small star from white icing, using the star cutter. Leave the star and stable to harden for 48 hours.

4   To make the various figures, colour the remaining sugarpaste as follows: 90g (3¼oz) purple, 90g (3¼oz) red, 90g (3¼oz) pale pink (using a dash of red colouring), 90g (3¼oz) grey (using a little black colouring), 60g (2¼oz) dark blue, 60g (2¼oz) pale blue and 30g (1¼oz) green. Leave 30g (1¼oz) white, then colour the remainder yellow.

5   Reserve 90g (3¼oz) of the yellow sugarpaste. Roll the remainder into a thick sausage shape. Dot with 30g (1¼oz) of the brown sugarpaste. Fold the ends of the sugarpaste into the centre and roll again so that the yellow sugarpaste becomes marbled with the brown (see page 30 for instructions). Continue rolling and folding until the colours are fairly evenly distributed throughout the whole piece of paste. Roll out the marbled sugarpaste and use to cover the cake and board. Trim off excess sugarpaste around the edges of the board with a sharp knife.

Dot the yellow sugarpaste with brown sugarpaste and roll together.

Make the stable using brown sugarpaste, following the templates.

6 To shape a 'king', make a small piece of purple-coloured sugarpaste into a cone shape. Shape two curved sections for the arms and secure to the cone. Shape head and hands from pink sugarpaste. For the cloak, cut a 5cm (2in) circle of sugarpaste using the large cutter. Cut away an area for the neck, and position around the body. Shape a small circle of brown sugarpaste for the hair, then add the crown and simple modelled gifts. Shape two more kings in the same way using different coloured sugarpaste.

7 Shape 'Mary' as above, draping a 4cm (1½in) circle of dark blue sugarpaste over her head.

8 Shape the remaining characters in the same way, using a piece of dried spaghetti for the centre of the shepherd's crook. For Jesus in the manger, shape a simple base of brown icing. Roll a tiny ball of flesh-coloured icing for the head and lay it on a thinly rolled square of white icing. Wrap the white icing around the head and lay it on the base. Paint facial details with a fine paintbrush and diluted brown food colouring.

9 For the donkey, mould the grey sugarpaste into a thick cylinder for the body, a teardrop shape for the head, flattened teardrops for the ears, 4 legs and a tail. Secure together so the donkey is in a sitting position, using sugar glue or royal icing.

10 Mix the icing sugar with a little water to make a paste. Colour it dark brown and place in a piping bag. Snip off the tip. Pipe a little icing down one side of the stable back. Secure one side-piece to the back and position on the cake. Position the other side-piece and then the roof sections in the same way. Pipe another line of icing around the base of the stable.

11 Use a little more icing to pipe the donkey's mane. Secure the star to the stable roof. Using a little diluted brown colouring, paint simple features onto the faces then position the figures on the cake.

12 Tie the cream cord around the cake and secure at the back with a little royal icing. Secure the ribbon around the edge of the cake board using a non-toxic glue stick to fix in place.

Make each king from a cone shape with a ball for the head.

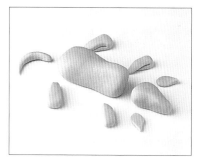

Make the donkey from grey sugarpaste shapes and arrange in a sitting position.

Pipe brown icing along the stable sides and roof to join.

AQUA ZOOM

Water chutes or flumes are now a highlight of many leisure pools. This cake should appeal to most children, even if they have never had a go on one.

1   Level the surface of the cake by cutting off any peak that formed during the baking process. Using a large, sharp knife, cut the cake in half from one top edge to the opposite lower edge. Turn the upper piece round so that the thin sides are together, creating a slope.

2   Using a knife, cut out an inverted 'S' shape from the cake. Reserve one of the large trimmed sections.

3   Use a third of the buttercream and 4 tbsp of the jam to sandwich the split cakes together. Press the remaining jam through a sieve to remove any pieces, then brush it over both pieces of the cake.

4   Place the large cake towards the back of the square cake board. Roll out 1kg (2¼lb) of the sugarpaste (rolled fondant) on a surface dusted with icing (confectioner's) sugar to a 36cm (14in) circle.

5   Lay this over the large cake and smooth down the sides with the palms of your hands and a smoother, easing it to fit. Trim off excess sugarpaste around the base using a sharp knife.

6   Use the trimmings and another 375g (13oz) sugarpaste to cover the small piece of cake. Place on the cake board.

7   Using a fine paintbrush and diluted blue food colouring, paint the sides of the cakes with stripes for a tiled effect. Mark the position of the stripes first with a cocktail stick (toothpick) to make sure the stripes run in neat parallel wavy lines and to enhance the tiled effect.

8   Colour another 275g (13oz) sugarpaste blue. Roll a little under the palms of your hands to form a long sausage. Secure this down the centre of the large cake,

CAKE AND DECORATION

23cm (9in) square
Madeira cake

500g (1lb 2oz) buttercream

7 tbsp strawberry or
raspberry jam

2kg (4¼lb) sugarpaste
(rolled fondant)

icing (confectioner's) sugar
for dusting

blue, flesh, red, green and
yellow food colourings

greenery, e.g. palm trees,
foliage

miniature paper umbrellas

SPECIAL EQUIPMENT

33cm (13in) square silver
cake board

Cut an inverted 'S' shape from the trimmed cake using a large sharp knife.

Mark the positions for the blue stripes on the edges of the cake.

then press all along to a point. Roll out the remaining blue icing and cut out two strips, each 30 x 7.5cm (12 x 3in).

10 Dampen the flat surface of the cake. Fit one blue sugarpaste strip down the side of the chute, so that one side rests on the blue ridge in the centre. Curve the other side of the strip up, supporting it, if necessary, with crumpled absorbent kitchen paper until the sugarpaste hardens. Position the second strip on the other side of the chute.

11 Set aside 2 tbsp of the remaining buttercream, and colour the rest blue. To create the look of moving water, spread the blue sugarpaste over the board with a palette knife, peaking it in some areas. Spread a thin covering of blue buttercream down the chute. Using the back of a spoon or palette knife, peak the blue buttercream around and down the chutes with the reserved white buttercream.

12 To make the figures, colour half the remaining sugarpaste with flesh colouring. (Modelling paste can be used if preferred.) A dot of red food colouring can be used to create a 'flesh' colour, if necessary. Roll a little to a thin sausage, about 6cm (2½in) long. Flatten slightly, then make a 2cm (¾in) cut from each end towards the centre. Mould the cut sections into outstretched arms and legs.

13 Place the figure halfway down one of the chutes. Roll out a small ball of flesh-coloured sugarpaste into a head and then paint a swimsuit on the body using a fine paintbrush.

14 Make more figures in the same way. For the boy leaving the chute, support the back with a cocktail stick, then lean it against the chute with the feet touching the water.

15 Shape two or three 'head and shoulder' figures in the water. Add hair using coloured sugarpaste.

16 Use the remaining sugarpaste to shape extra decorations, such as a beach ball. Add palm trees, or other foliage, as required; either use bought items or model trees from green and brown modelling paste. Arrange the miniature paper umbrellas round about.

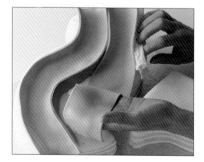

Position the blue strips so that one side rests on the blue ridge in the centre.

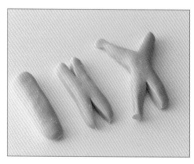

Make the figures from flesh sugarpaste, arranging the limbs as required.

TEMPLATES

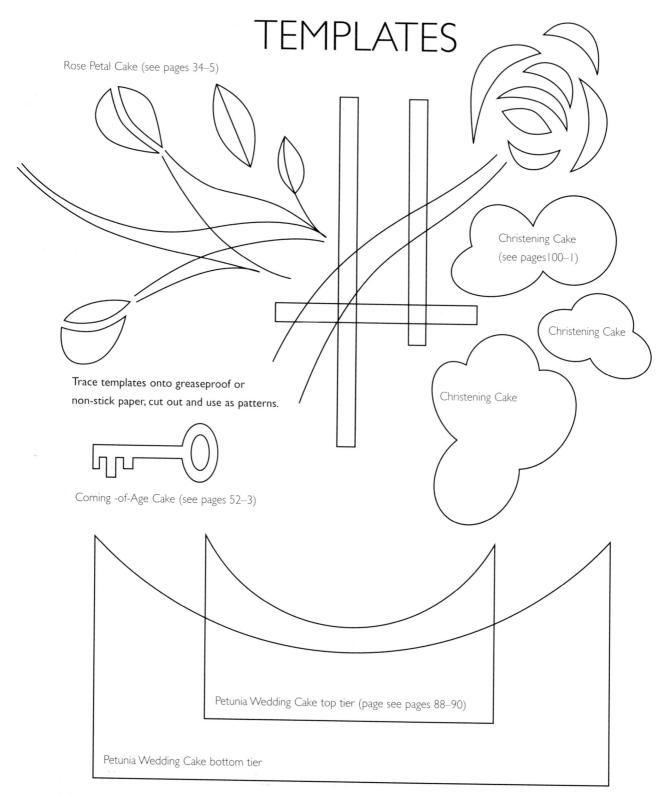

Rose Petal Cake (see pages 34–5)

Christening Cake
(see pages100–1)

Christening Cake

Christening Cake

Trace templates onto greaseproof or
non-stick paper, cut out and use as patterns.

Coming -of-Age Cake (see pages 52–3)

Petunia Wedding Cake top tier (page see pages 88–90)

Petunia Wedding Cake bottom tier

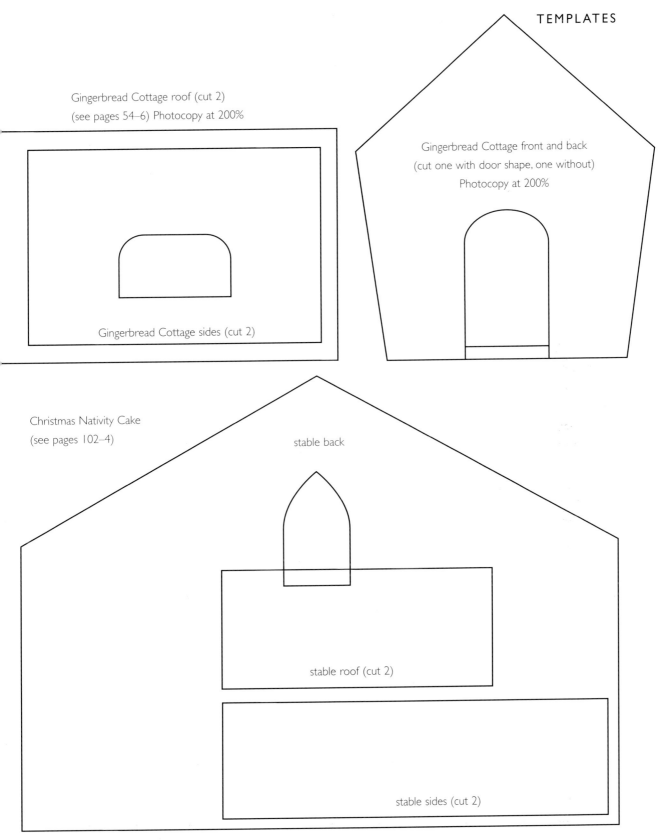

Gingerbread Cottage roof (cut 2)
(see pages 54–6) Photocopy at 200%

Gingerbread Cottage front and back
(cut one with door shape, one without)
Photocopy at 200%

Gingerbread Cottage sides (cut 2)

Christmas Nativity Cake
(see pages 102–4)

stable back

stable roof (cut 2)

stable sides (cut 2)

Teddy Gâteau
(see pages 66–7)

Clown Cake (see pages 42–3)

Floodwork Flowers (see pages 57–9)

SUPPLIERS

UK

Celcakes and Celcrafts
Springfield House
Gate Helmsley, York
Yorkshire TO4 1NF
Tel. 01759 371447

Confectionery Supplies (CS)
27 Eign Road
Hereford HR1 2RU
Tel. 01432 271200

Culpitt Cake Art
Culpitt Ltd
Jubilee Industrial Estate
Ashington
Northumberland NE63 8UQ
Tel. 01670 814545

Fine Cut Cutters (FCC)
Workshop 2, Old Stable Block
Holme Pierrepoint Hall
Nottingham NG12 2LD
Tel. 0115 933 4349

Guy, Paul & Co. Ltd
Unit B4, Foundry Way
Little End Road
Eaton Socon
Cambs. PE19 3JH

Holly Products (HP)
Holly Cottage
Hassall Green
Sandbach
Cheshire CW11 0YA
Tel. 01270 761403

Kit Box (KB)
DRF Technical Services
1 Fernlea Gardens
Easton in Gordano
Avon BS20 0JF
Tel. & Fax. 01275 374557

Orchard Products (OP)
51 Hallyburton Road
Hove
East Sussex BN3 7GP
Tel. 01273 419418
Fax. 01273 412512

Patchwork Cutters (PC)
3 Raines Close
Greasby, Wirral
Merseyside CH49 2QB
Tel./Fax. 0151 678 5053

PME Sugarcraft (PME)
Brember Road
South Harrow
Middlesex HA2 8UN
Tel. 020 8864 0888

Renshaw Scott Ltd
Crown Street
Liverpool L8 7RF
Tel. 0151 706 8200
(Renshaw Regalice sugarpaste)

Squires Kitchen
Squires House
3 Waverley Lane
Farnham
Surrey GU9 8BB
Tel. 01252 711749

FRANCE

Artgato
5 Avenue du
Arnold Netter
75012 Paris

AUSTRALIA

Cake Decorating School of Australia
Shop 7, Port Philip Arcade
232 Flinders Street
Melbourne
Victoria 3000
Tel. + 61 3 9654 5335

Cupid's Cake Decorations
2/90 Belford Street
Broadmeadow
NSW 2292
Tel. +61 2 4962 1884

USA

Beryl's Cake Decorating
& Pastry Supplies
PO Box 1584
N. Springfield
VA22151–0584
Tel. +1 800 488 2749

Nicholas Lodge
International Sugar Art Collection
6060 McDonough Drive, Suite D
Norcross, GA 30093
Tel. +1 770 453 9449

CANADA

Creative Cutters
561 Edward Avenue,
Unit 1,
Richmond Hill
Ontario L4C 9W6
Tel. +1 905 883 5638

SOUTH AFRICA

JEM Cutters (J)
PO Box 115 Kloof 3640
Kwazulu Natal
Tel. +27 31 7011431

WEST AFRICA

Kogsy Sugarcraft Centre
Rikaz Plaza, 58 Opebi Road
Ikeja Lagos
Tel. 00234 1 8965790

16 Bankole Street
Oke Arin Lagos

A15 LSDPC Shopping Centre
Adeniran Ogunsanya Street
Surulere Lagos, Nigeria
Tel. 00234 1 4396611, 8973214

INDEX

First published in 2002 by
Murdoch Books Pty Limited

This edition published in 2007.
Reprinted 2008.

Copyright 2002 © Murdoch Books Pty Limited

Murdoch Books Australia
Pier 8/9, 23 Hickson Road
Millers Point NSW 2000
Tel: +61 (0) 2 8220 2000
Fax: +61 (0) 2 8220 2558

Murdoch Books UK Limited
Erico House, 6th Floor
93-99 Upper Richmond Road
Putney, London SW15 2TG
Tel: +44 (0) 20 8355 1480
Fax: +44 (0) 20 8355 1499

Chief Executive: Juliet Rogers
Publisher: Kay Scarlett

Commissioning Editor: Barbara Croxford
Editorial: Grapevine Publishing Services Ltd
Design and templates: Stuart Perry
Managing Editor: Anna Osborn
Design Manager: Helen Taylor
Senior Production Controller: Kirsty Gibson
Photo Librarian: Bobbie Leah

ISBN 978 174196 052 5
Cataloguing-in-Publication Data is available
from the National Library of Australia.

A catalogue record of this book is available
from the British Library.

Colour separation by Colourscan, Singapore
Printed by Tien Wah Press, Singapore, 2007.